Education and Values

by the same author

FREEDOM AND AUTHORITY IN EDUCATION

EDUCATION IN AN INDUSTRIAL SOCIETY

EDUCATION AND VALUES

Essays in the theory of education

G. H. BANTOCK

FABER AND FABER
24 Russell Square
London

First published in mcmlxv
by Faber and Faber Limited
24 Russell Square London WC1
Second impression mcmlxvii
Printed in Great Britain by
Billing & Sons Limited
Guildford and London

*Action is consolatory. It is the enemy of thought
and the friend of flattering illusions.*

Conrad: *Nostromo*

Contents

Acknowledgments

A number of these essays have been published previously in various journals; and I am indebted to the editors of the following for permission to reprint: *British Journal of Educational Studies*, *Educational Review*, *Education for Teaching*, *Harvard Educational Review*. The initial year of publication is appended to those essays which are here reprinted; some have undergone minor alterations.

I was, as ever, indebted to T. S. Eliot for his interest and advice; his death is to me a sharp, personal blow because his support of my work has sustained me in views which are neither fashionable nor popular at the moment. Mr. S. J. Eggleston of the Leicester University School of Education kindly read and commented on the essay 'Education, Social Justice and the Sociologists', though I must take responsibility for the opinions therein expressed. I am most grateful to my wife for her work in typing and preparing the manuscript and index.

G. H. B.

Rearsby, Leicestershire

Introduction

These essays are the products of a mind which, in so far as it has been trained at all, has been exercised on literature, supplemented by a little philosophy. The tradition of literary criticism to which I belong and the modern philosophy in which I have been interested, are both characterized by a close attention to language, which is why some of the essays indulge in a certain amount of close analysis. Educational discourse, as I pointed out some years ago, is marked by a good deal of vagueness; and it has not yet encountered in this country much of that linguistic therapy which modern philosophy has provided in other fields. Though what I have to say no doubt involves its own confusions and ambiguities, it is a matter of regret to me that I have encountered so little in the way of challenge to a more complete elucidation and clarification; for part of the strengthening of a discipline springs from the clash of minds, the co-operation of opposing interpretations, the rigorous attempt to expose error. Educational writing has for long suffered from a distressing lack of precision, one moreover which pervades most of the relevant fields. To attempt a clearer thinking, however badly in practice it may be accomplished, seems to me to be worth the effort, even if only to stimulate to a repudiation.

But a linguistic therapy is not in itself enough, though it may constitute an essential propaedeutic. Education aims to transmit aspects of human experience to the as yet uninitiated, and so involves an introduction to modes of behaviour—which certainly include modes of thinking and feeling—relevant to our common life. The educationist is unavoidably a moralist, by the very logic of his position. He must make choices, whether on a basis of habit or as a result of rational assessment, and by the latter method particularly in a civilization which increasingly prides itself on the extension of decision-making which has marked its progress. Habit, indeed, is increasingly in disfavour and rational, conscious choice more and more the approved mode. There is no escaping this extension of consciousness, and certainly not by the educationist who is being made ever more aware of the tools at his disposal through the efforts of a steadily increasing band of research workers. Hence his choices become subject to argument; and when they rest on tacit assumptions or act as the initial yet undisclosed stimulus to research attention, they are the better for being revealed so that they can be discussed.

And so the educator is inevitably involved in the world of values; and here, it seems to me, literature provides some measure of protection against many of those over-simplifications of outlook and procedure which mar so much of current educational discourse. There is, for instance, a good deal of talk about education for living; but the living implicit in the formulation seems all too frequently inadequate or insufficiently in touch with psychic and social realities. It is not only that literary artists have done a great deal to give actuality to the complexities of human behaviour; it is also that through the choices they make they display a peculiarly sensitive awareness of human finenesses and possibilities. They tap levels of consciousness most educationists ignore; and consciousness (of a sort) is specifically the aim of our cognitively-based Western educational system.

The more precise nature of an intelligence fostered on literature I have tried to define in the essay 'Education and the Literary Intelligence'; what, in the main, I find significant about this form of intelligence is the peculiar combination of intellect and emotion with which it penetrates human experience. It is in these terms that I offer an extended analysis of Rousseau's *Emile*. Rousseau has long been thought the father of the romantic sensibility; but, judged against the best products of the literary intelligence, his work seems to comprise only an abstract and too logical statement of a projected human development, of which the obverse side is provided by a distressing romantic sentimentality. Nevertheless, Rousseau occupies a peculiarly important position in modern educational ideology. If anyone deserves to be termed the father of progressivism, it is he; and, although progressivism is, in general, rather out of favour now, it yet exerts a great deal of influence over some aspects of our educational system. It is, in any case, a more interesting subject for educational controversy than that which has replaced it in public and pedagogical attention, the concern for system and organization: at least it takes us closer to the classroom and the child in it.

But Rousseau also raises in an easily assimilable way some very fundamental educational problems, especially in the field of method and pupil-teacher relationships. What could be more provocative in the matter of bringing up children than his statement: 'He [i.e. Emile] should only do what he wants to do; but he should only want to do what you want him to do.' Here is revealed a central equivocation implicit in much progressive practice—the promulgation of freedom in a situation which inevitably involves an element of authority. Rousseau, indeed, demonstrates that those who affect to despise the works of the Great Educators are, in some cases at least, wrong to do so. As Mr. John Plamenatz has recently shown in the field of political philosophy, the ideas of past thinkers of this stature have a relevance to current controversies, partly because we depend in our thinking about ultimate principles and values on what our great predecessors have taught us and partly because these ideas are nowhere more clearly and cogently expressed than in their writings. As Mr. Plamenatz puts it when speaking of his own field: 'The great advantage of these old theories is that they are both rich in content and familiar. . . . Everyone agrees that students of society and government need to look carefully at the assumptions they make and the ideas they use; that they, owing to the nature of their subject, are especially liable to be the dupes of words. . . . It is therefore a point worth making, that these ideas are nowhere better or more economically studied than in these old theories' (Introduction to *Man and Society*)

The same, it seems to me, is true of past theorists of education. The same issues tend to recur from generation to generation; and, if we penetrate beneath the surface of Rousseau's fable, we can find some of them stated there. So, even if we do not necessarily agree with Rousseau's solutions, we must be grateful to him for facing us with many of the actualities of the educative situation. In any case, his sentimental aspirations, his sheer belief in the possibilities of education, have entered deeply into our consciousness. Although it was actually Helvetius who said 'L'éducation peut tout', the words could as easily have been written by Rousseau. His anti-historical bent, for instance, reappears among the assumptions made by our contemporary environmentalists. Like him, they expect to transcend the shaping power of historical forces by adjustments in the environment. Rousseau's perfectionism, in fact, is part of our modern experience, and we share something of his apocalyptic naïvety.

So, in the sense that he raised fundamental issues which are still with us, Rousseau is important; and equally important are the limitations of the mind he brought to bear on their solution. I have tried to bring these out. In the past, I have sometimes been accused of being too negative in my approach, too critical, too little concerned with positive affirmation. It is not for me to deny this criticism; but I may, at least, be allowed to urge that in educational thinking as I have briefly described it above, negative criticism has a very positive role to play. There is so much loose thinking to be cleared away before we can see our educational problems clearly; and nowhere is this more so than in the vexed question of the relationship between education and the social order of which it forms a part. Some of the dilemmas involved I have dealt with in my recently published *Education in an Industrial Society*; but I hope that the essay on Mannheim and Durkheim, two of the most important social theorists of education, will provide other clarifications.

As a further example of the sort of verbal therapy I have in mind, I have included an extended study of the concept of freedom in education, a notion which owes much of its currency to Rousseau and which deserves some consideration in its social and historical context. Here, the important ambiguity is that between 'freedom from' and 'freedom to'; and the nature of the particular freedom we have in mind has its immediate relevance in concrete decisions to be taken in the classroom. Such considerations are particularly important in assessing the position of the teacher. There may be certain contexts in which he can best foster growth by standing aside; in others, he needs to fulfil his moral role in a positive manner, by taking a very specific stand and by seeking to exert a very direct influence. The relationship of teacher and taught is essentially a dynamic one and cannot be reduced to a formula; varying circumstances, different subject matter requires different modes of treatment; and it is a matter of tact on the teacher's part to know when interference is essential and when it could be harmful. But the logic of the situation demands that it shall be *his* decision about what to do, for he is inescapably in a position where it is necessary for him to take decisions, both about what to do and about how to do it—the connection between the two will be close, of course.

Hence the teacher, as I have indicated, is inescapably involved in the world of values. Whatever psychological and sociological facts may be at his disposal, it is still his decision as to which set of facts he chooses to pay most attention to. Again, one of the dilemmas of the educational investigator is that he will necessarily have to choose to investigate this, rather than that, topic of interest as a result of prior assumptions of value and relevance. One of the dangers of being too much guided by educational research, for instance, is that it may lead us unwittingly to accept what are, in effect, implicit value judgments of cogency and importance. Our priorities will be influenced by other people's, often unconscious, value judgments concerning what it is most important to find out—a good example being the current concern about class rather than, say, about pop culture, because the sociologist has taught us to be aware of the effects of the one much more than he has directed our attention to the other—a theme of my essay on 'Education, Social Justice and the Sociologists'. I would like, too, to regard my essay on 'Fact and Value in Education' as having a relevance wider than simply to the work of Susan Isaacs with which it is ostensibly concerned; for one of the problems of our times arises out of the way in which our thinking is being influenced by the value assumptions of social and psychological investigators. In so far as they themselves accept current valuations (and most of them, in this respect, are highly conventional, as witness the research implicit in Robbins) they may, though largely unaware of what they are doing, encourage us to neglect aspects of the personality or social possibilities which, in relation to the deeper psychic 'needs' (in itself a value loaded word) of the times deserve much more attention than they receive.

Here, also, the literary intelligence has its part to play. For, in general, it has fallen to the lot of literary writers to utter the more relevant protests against the preoccupations of the age and the shortcomings of the society we are inhabiting. Because of their greater psychic awareness of the complexities of human beings, their bringing into play neglected features of the personality, they can contribute to a sounder view of what constitutes a healthy society than is implicit in the materialist pressures of the times; for, what such pressures imply is some degree of psychic impoverishment—an impoverishment reflected in the nature of much popular (and often, of supposedly sophisticated) art. The literary artist can contribute, then, to the *range* of morality implicit in the educative process, and help us to appreciate aims and purposes more fully. Furthermore, he can often aid the very process of definition in the previously accepted field of research by sensitizing us to aspects of relevant human affairs that blunter sensibilities may miss. I have made this clear in my criticism of educational research. Here, the philosophical question: 'What sort of research is educational research?' encounters a possibility which might have been obvious from the start to someone trained in literature—that many (though not all) of the questions we ask about human behaviour are likely to imply different procedures of investigation from those required in the investigation of physical matter; and that a good deal of educational research fails in its aims because it seeks to measure what is not quantifiable with the same degree of accuracy as can be the behaviour of inanimate objects. It encounters, too, the need for a conceptual clarification of a language which is usually demotic, not technical, in its reference to human affairs.

In general, then, these essays are intended as reminders that judgments about value are essential to the educator, both as the unconscious background to his enterprise and in the day-to-day conscious decision taking which is essential at many levels in a national system of education. That is why the essay, 'What is Wrong with English Education', in a sense, forms the key to the whole collection. For what is centrally wrong with English education is its unwillingness to face up to the need for raising questions of value, translated into specific curricular requirements. So many educationists spend their time finding, often rather dubious, answers to not always very well framed questions, or asking factual questions in fields of which a profounder vision of human existence might have queried the relevance and importance. Of course, we want as many relevant facts as we can find; but, amidst current preoccupations, some emphasis on the need to consider problems of value (which is a different thing from actually legislating about what people ought to do) is surely a prime necessity.

Underlying the present collection, I hope I can detect a consistent viewpoint—a consistency the outward symbols of which are the references, direct or implied, to those who have done a great deal to form my own thinking and who fulfil, therefore, something of the function that Matthew Arnold assigned to his 'touchstones'. I do not altogether regret some repetition of reference—it seems to indicate that, despite the disparity of theme and subject matter, these essays are all the product of a single mind working within a specific frame of reference.

I have referred to this compilation as 'Essays in the Theory of

Education'. The word 'theory' is taken from a Greek word which means a 'viewing'. In a fairly loose usage it implies a general contemplation of the problems relating to a particular field of activity and has therefore, to my mind, a wider implication than the term 'philosophy of education' which today has a very specific technical application. Many of the essays are explicitly philosophical, but not all of them—and I have therefore preferred the term of wider implication. Furthermore, it should be realized that the background of the earlier essays implied a greater interest in theoretical progressivism than is manifest today, when our interests have become more administrative and social.

What is Wrong with English Education?[1]

When we educate, we inevitably work in terms of certain assumptions about human potentiality and human good; behind the practices we approve or the recommendations we make lie usually unexpressed views on the nature and functioning of mind, on the variety and scope of human 'need' in development, on the relative value to be assigned to different areas of 'knowledge'. These views remain tacit rather than explicit because too often our day-to-day purposes and practices arise out of some felt social requirement or some immediate pressure to conform; education is, in some connotation of the phrase, too much of a social process not to invite pragmatic tinkerings or proximate interferences. It comes easily under the influence of politics, and politics is notoriously subject to the pressures of the market-place, where the bustle of daily business inhibits the questioning of assumption and purpose.

Yet, it seems to me peculiarly the function of a university to provide a milieu within which it is possible to try to lay bare the deeper implications of our actions, to ask the more fundamental questions. And that is why I do not want to ask the question: 'What is wrong with English education?' in terms simply of organization and administration, of half-subjects added, or quarter-subjects dropped, of eleven plus or of eighteen plus, or of any of those proximate questions which delight the journalist and the propagandist. I prefer to make the attempt—however

[1] Lecture given to the Haldane Society of the University of Leicester, somewhat revised.

inadequately I may carry it out—to ask some questions about the nature and value of the education we provide in terms which will allow me to suggest inadequacies profounder than those implicit in temporary social exigency.

The first thing, I think, to notice—and it is something so accepted that its extraordinary incidence goes unremarked—is that this education is compulsory and is intended to lead to universal literacy. I know of no previous civilization which has attempted to impose on all its denizens the necessity of learning to read and write; and, even in ours, compulsion has lasted for less than a hundred years. Furthermore, this education takes place in institutions specially set apart for the purpose, whereas in the past a great deal of education has taken place within the family circle or within small family-like groups, such as those of apprenticeship under a domestic economy, or in the training in courtesy provided in a great house. This, of course, is partly because of the numbers involved in a mass society; but it is also partly because of the nature of the education involved. The education we provide in these institutions is one which involves the gradual internalization of highly complicated ways of fashioning our common world, so that we can arrive at some measure of understanding of it; and, by and large, this understanding is of a sort that involves *conscious* awareness, the result of reflection and research. The elaboration of this 'understanding' has been going on for centuries, and, by its very nature, has necessitated a division into a separately defined and periodically increased number of subject-fields, where the proliferation of knowledge has required increasingly specialized treatment. Ideally regarded, these subject-fields have been the means through which we have come to understand the world of nature, that of man in society, and the internal world of the passions and moral choice. And their characteristic features are those of consciousness and understanding.

Their appeal, indeed, is largely to intellectual processes; even that field concerned most with man's inner world, the study of literature, all too often misses the affective core implicit in literature's ordering of the passions and concentrates on the less essential elements of contemporary reference or biographical detail; as Yeats put it:

> *Bald heads forgetful of their sins,*
> *Old, learned, respectable bald heads*
> *Edit and annotate the lines*
> *That young men, tossing on their beds,*
> *Rhymed out in love's despair*
> *To flatter beauty's ignorant ear.*

It is entirely typical of such a situation that, when the greatest of child psychologists, Jean Piaget, expounds his earlier developmental theories and chronicles the progress of developing consciousness in the child, he should do so in terms that imply a basic split between what he terms 'autistic or dream thought' and intelligent activity. The former is not adapted to reality, but creates for itself a 'dream-world of imagination', one essentially individualistic and 'obeying a whole system of special laws' (laws of symbolism and of immediate satisfaction); but what he terms 'intelligent apprehension' is adapted to reality, and is essentially the result of socialization. And the 'reality' implicit in these definitions is that of logical deduction and empirical investigation, the world of hypotheses and the world of observation; the rest is 'whim', 'dream', 'imagination'. And in this, of course, he is much influenced—he consciously alludes to it—by the theory of knowledge implicit in Freudian psychology, with its basic split between the 'reality' and the 'pleasure' principles. Here art 'does not seek to be anything else but an illusion', 'it never dares to make any attacks on the realm of reality'.[1]

In this, Freud and Piaget—the two greatest influences on the development of child psychology of our times—simply reflect their period; they are themselves the product of assumptions they have tended to reinforce. Basically, and simply, these involve a view analogous to that expressed by T. S. Eliot, that

[1] *New Introductory Lectures.* Elsewhere Freud allows art to have *some* contact with reality; but, in general, this quotation seems to represent his general picture. His clinical practice, perhaps, implies a different view.

what has taken place in the modern consciousness is a split between the emotional and intellectual aspects of the mind—a split Eliot has himself celebrated under the title of 'dissociation of sensibility', and the beginnings of which he has located in the seventeenth century. It is a notion which has been under attack from Professor Frank Kermode; but, whatever may be true of its historical origins, I persist in finding in it a rough and ready guide to the elucidation of certain aspects of the modern consciousness; the countervailing emphasis in Yeats's stress on Unity of Being comes as an important corrective in conceiving the ills implicit in modern education.

For, of course, the sort of education we provide bears witness to the prevailing assumptions about the nature of consciousness and its objects; and shortcomings in the one will be reflected in shortcomings in the other. You will, perhaps, be gathering that all this constitutes a prologue to the judgment that our education is over-intellectualized; and, in a sense, this is so. But here we must be careful; these concepts of 'intellect' and 'emotion' are essentially slippery and ill-conceived. The concept of 'emotion', particularly, is extraordinarily vague and ill-defined, as Mr. James Hillman has convincingly demonstrated in a volume exclusively devoted to examining the confusions to be found among psychologists' and philosophers' uses of the word. If, then, I urge a greater emphasis on emotional education I do so with the full awareness that the precise nature of the emotions is in some doubt,[1] and that the relationship between emotion and intellect requires rigorous conceptual clarification. Certainly, what I have *not* got in mind is that emphasis to be found in much 'progressive' theory on a sort of spontaneous self-expression as a means to therapy; for what I would want to recommend is not a form of self-release and therapy, but a mode of structuring, a means to order, an elaboration and a making; and the emphasis should be, not on the self, but on the product. Furthermore, this making, at whatever level it exists, in itself involves various sorts of knowledge; it is a romantic

[1] A comprehensive study of theories of emotion will be found in James Hillman, *Emotion.*

fallacy to think that creativity in any sphere can be mindless—as Professor Edgar Wind has convincingly shown in his recent *Art and Anarchy*.

There is nothing especially new, here, of course, in my bringing to the fore the need for emotional education. A good deal of it can be found in Plato. But it needs to be worked out at a level which will meet the positivistic challenge. What I require, in fact, is a theory of mind and an aesthetic that see in artistic creation a means to elaboration and structuring analogous to, and as essential to human development as, that implicit in those processes of empirical investigation and logical deduction we term science. It is here, I think, that we come to the heart of the two cultures controversy, which is one of the basic issues in education of our times. It is not that the arts and sciences are necessarily incompatible or basically antagonistic pursuits; rather, they fulfil different roles in the development of the complete human being. This is not to say that a too exclusive emphasis on the one may not act in detriment of the other; our world is dominated by science to the extent that our notions of 'truth' and the aura of emotional satisfaction which such a concept carries with it are derived in the main, from what is empirically verifiable or tautologous. It may very well be that in our education we should do more to nurture neglected aspects of that syncretism[1] which Piaget describes as constituting an essential stage in child development; that the process of 'objectification' from egocentrism in which he sees the ideal course of development to logico-empirical modes of thought needs refining by concentration on other, more affectively based modes of apprehension; so that the particular progress towards what Piaget calls 'objectification'—which is, roughly,

[1] *Syncretism:* refers to that characteristic of child thought which tends to juxtapose logically unrelated pieces of information when the child is asked, for instance, for causal explanations. It may lead to the fusing of images according to laws which are similar to those implicit in the Freudian 'condensation' of dream images rather than to those of logic. A simple example would be: 'Why does the sun not fall down?' 'Because it is hot. The sun stops there' 'How?' 'Because it is yellow.' But this phase of thought may be important in the development of metaphor.

science—is seen as only one possible mode of development implicit in childish egocentrism—there are other modes of objectification.

Now, I find implicit in the works of Ernst Cassirer and explicit in those of his pupil, Professor Susanne Langer, a much more satisfactory treatment of consciousness which would allow us to further the development of the emotions seriously, as it were, and not simply to regard them as tiresome nuisances which need to be sublimated in fantasy or repressed. Educationists—especially educational psychologists—are always appealing to the 'needs' of children; but all too often the assumptions about human needs to which they appeal are drawn from animal behaviour or a positivist philosophy. In fact, men's needs are unique, for they derive from what makes man unique, his capacity for symbolization: he is, in Cassirer's phrase: 'animal symbolicum'. And this leads to the appreciation that discursive discourse such as is found in modern science is only one of a number of symbolic modes of expression, and one which fulfils only a limited number of human potentialities: 'there is an unexplored possibility of genuine semantic beyond the limits of discursive language'—through, that is, non-discursive forms of symbolism; and Susanne Langer instances the importance of ritual, dance and art as forms of the articulation of *feelings* through non-discursive symbolic forms—what she calls presentational symbols—which nevertheless are manifestations of human rationality, ways, that is, in terms of which men have attempted to make sense of their environment. I cannot here enter on a detailed account of the aesthetic that Susanne Langer puts forward in her *Feeling and Form*. All I can do is to indicate that it involves an emphasis on the expressive function of art, of art as involving an *articulation* of feelings. It involves a process of *objectification*; and in this it goes far beyond progressive 'self-expressionism'. For what is expressed becomes central; and, as Susanne Langer puts it: 'Sheer self-expression requires no artistic form.' In her view, music, for instance, becomes the '*formulation and representation* of emotions, moods, mental tensions and resolutions—a "logical picture" of sentient, responsive life, a source of insight, not a plea for sympathy'. This constitutes a view which, to my mind, ties up with certain of the contemporaneous views of T. S. Eliot—particularly on the role of technique and his account of the *impersonality* of the artist; (I remember, too, his statement: 'every precise emotion tends towards intellectual formulation'); and it has affinities, also, with the critical practice of Dr. F. R. Leavis. The view I am putting forward can be summed up in the sentence: 'Art is the creation of forms symbolic of human feeling.'

The net effect of all this is to place artistic creativity as a human 'need' equal in importance to that represented by discursive thought. Myth, ritual, art take their places as centrally human activities expressive of human tendencies and potentialities as vital—and, in their own way, as disciplined—as intellectual, cognitive processes. Science appears as one important way of structuring the world; but positive knowledge based on physical facts is not the only way in which we meet the world; and a lack of attention to other modes of articulation and structuring, more affectively based, are ignored at our peril. We live in a world, as Susanne Langer points out, which presents '. . . two great threats to mental security: the new mode of living, which has made the old nature-symbols alien to our minds, and the new mode of working, which makes personal activity meaningless, inacceptable to the hungry imagination. Most men never see the goods they produce, but stand by a travelling belt and turn a million identical passing screws or close a million identical passing wrappers in a succession of hours, days, years. This sort of activity is too poor, too empty, for even the most ingenious mind to invest it with symbolic content. Work is no longer a sphere of ritual; and so the nearest and surest source of mental satisfaction has dried up.' It is here that the artistic indifference of our educational system is so crippling; for, more than anything else in experience, the arts mould our actual life of feeling; and crude art means crude feeling; to quote Susanne Langer again: 'People who are so concerned for their children's scientific enlightenment that they keep Grimm out of the library and Santa Claus out of the chimney, allow the cheapest art, the worst of bad singing, the most revolting sentimental fiction to impinge on the children's minds all day and every day, from infancy. If the rank and file of youth grows up in emotional cowardice and confusion, sociologists look to economic conditions or family relations for the cause of this deplorable "human weakness", but not to the ubiquitous influence of corrupt art, which steeps the average mind in a shallow sentimentalism that ruins what germs of true feeling might have developed in it.' It is not so much that we live in a world without art; indeed, there can never have been a time in the history of man when there has been such a plethora of artistic creation—of a sort. The decay of folk traditions has encouraged the development of a substitute, commercial 'culture' in a decadent romantic mode—as witness the 'pop' culture of our days. And this artistic tradition exercises an infinitely more potent effect on our youth than do their teachers. 'Art'—to quote Mrs. Langer again—'is a public possession, because the formulation of "felt life" is the heart of any culture and moulds the objective world for its people'.

Now, what is the relevance of all this to the problems of universal education? Affective education is as important as discursive education for all sections of the community, in the emotionally impoverished environment implied by so much of our popular culture. We need many more colleges of the arts to which our able people could go and in which they could study, for instance, the opportunities implicit in the mass media. Furthermore, we must confess that over eighty years of compulsory education have left us completely in the dark concerning a possible syllabus for the less able; what we provide at the moment is almost worse than useless—the watered-down grammar school syllabus constitutes a vain attempt to induct into high culture which leads to indifference or resentment; and any vocational bias is meaningless to those whose subsequent work can be learnt in an hour, a day or a week. Even allowing a greater potential for some of these children than their environment permits, the psychological inhibitions to the acquiring of even an adequate vocabulary to enable them to cope with 'high' culture—a point made by Bernstein[1]—means that we must, in some degree, work at the level of consciousness which this environment permits. Hence the radical reshaping of the syllabus I have recently suggested in terms of a training in rationality which will enable them to deal with the immediacy of personal and family decision in an informed manner, and a concern for affective and participatory possibilities which will give them some counter-balance to the gross infidelities of 'pop' culture.[2]

For, of course, the emphasis on secondary reorganization and on educational expansion at the behest largely of abstract socio-political notions, has, in general, conspicuously failed to face up to the question of content which is the fundamental question facing us in education today. As things stand, I can see little point in the immense proliferation of education with which we are threatened—though, ideally speaking, we should undergo such an expansion. But, before we undergo such an expansion there needs to be a great deal of basic thinking about the nature of the curriculum in relation to the various levels of consciousness with which we are faced; thinking, moreover, which takes into account a fuller realization of human need and potentiality than is implicit in the expansionist aims of our day, with their dreary associations of 'educated manpower' and 'Education; Our Untapped Wealth'; thinking, too, which faces up to the immense educational waste in terms of actual results which characterizes our present system.

This is not to say that the technical demands of the industrial-bureaucratic state should not be met; but the concern for status and examination success fostered by its proliferating needs suggests that, for instance, the educative potentialities of the great academic disciplines will not exercise their civilizing influence on the able to the full. The chief virtue of the notion of 'education for its own sake' rather than for some external incentive like an examination lies in the possibilities it affords of a full exploitation of subject material rather than a concentration on

[1] Cf. Basil Bernstein, 'Social Class and Linguistic Development', reprinted in *Education, Economy and Society*, ed. Halsey (Floud and Anderson).

[2] Cf. my *Education in an Industrial Society* (Faber, 1963).

the more technically assessable aspects of disciplines. Though human motives are essentially mixed, and the preliminary incentive of a grading examination may often have provided the initial impulse for what has turned out to be a lifelong interest as well as a paper qualification, it also happens that the subject merely becomes a vehicle for a journey in a further stage of the rat-race.

And, indeed, here we touch on one of the characteristic stresses to which modern education is subjected. In the past, education has been related to function and has frequently taken on significance in relation to work. The division of labour and other forms of specialization at a variety of levels have led to the introduction of an education that is abstracted from the pressures of living, one which exists in the terms mooted by the nineteenth century of faculty development and an abstract mental training. It was out of this situation that the protest of John Dewey arose. Looked at from one point of view, Dewey's whole work involves an attempt to find motives for learning which would appeal in a situation where the traditional motives no longer operate. But Dewey's error was twofold; he failed to take the full measure of the industrial-bureaucratic state and the psychic impoverishment it involved—whatever potentialities it may have provided; and he was obsessed by democratic-egalitarian notions (he isn't the only one, of course) which have only a very limited potential in the essentially meritocratic structure that faced him. But, in a sense, his problem is ours; what motives for learning will appeal to a polyglot collection of young people drawn from a variety of social strata faced by the demands of a culture which is often foreign to them and their forbears?

This is a socio-cultural problem of immense significance for the future of our civilization which, so far as I can see, only T. S. Eliot has tried to face in his *Notes towards the Definition of Culture*; but Eliot's solution in terms of the preservation of an hereditary class as opposed to a status hierarchy implicit in a meritocratic society is not a feasible one at this stage of social development. What the solution is I can only hint at—that we should exploit in schools positive aspects of this century's characteristic cultural forms—film, radio, TV, etc., otherwise I cannot believe much in the cultural potentialities implicit in a machine technology. It is, of course, arguable that a machine technology is one aspect of our culture, both in its own right and in the aesthetic problems of design it raises. This is true; and it accounts for the fact that 'design' is perhaps one of the few areas of artistic activity to flourish in our times. But I believe that the too great emphasis on technical proficiency such as we now witness (it is, of course, a matter of degree, for all civilizations have had their technical aids) will lead to the decay of artistic traditions—has, in fact, perhaps already done so—because of the restlessness engendered, the excessive stimulation of the desire to control, the substitution of mechanical for human rhythms, the basic scepticism implicit in scientific and technical advance. It is no longer possible to live in divided and distinguished worlds when one of the two worlds has so patently triumphed; and it is my aim to redress a balance.

My contention, then, is that the terms in which any mooted expansion exists fail to recognize these sorts of problems. Education, of course, as Eliot pointed out, is itself a cultural manifestation; it is not, in general, a means to cultural initiation but, in large degree, reflects the stresses and pressures of the society it serves to perpetuate. Nevertheless, in so far as education itself is subject to moral choice, it is always open to human beings—if only isolated human beings in particular classrooms—to challenge prevailing modes; hence, a deeper analysis of educational deficiencies, however much it may go against current conceptions of social 'need', is not an entirely fruitless undertaking.

And this brings me to my last point in relation to what is wrong with English education—the low level at which educational discussion is frequently carried on. I remember the shock I got a few years ago when a distinguished academic said to me that, of course, 'education' as studied in university had become largely a technical subject. The notion seemed to tie in so little with my own preoccupations with education that, for a moment, I was even at a loss to understand what he meant. Then, of course, I came to realize that, to a large extent, he was right—'education' had become increasingly a matter of research into child development and learning theory, into implication for social structure and the effects of social environment, into method and teaching aids, into backwardness and special school problems, into organization and administration. It had, in fact, developed into a technology, into a set of theoretical structures designed to facilitate the achievement of defined ends; its aim was efficiency.

Now, I have no *a priori* objection to efficiency;[1] and we certainly do need to improve the quality of our teaching and our understanding of the processes at work as people learn, etc. We do need to find out more facts about the educational situation; we do need to know a great deal more about the actual effects it has in our society. And so, I regard this technical development in the educational sphere without animus—though, incidentally with a certain measure of scepticism as to whether it is, in fact, always being conducted in the best possible way. My doubts, here, indeed arise out of a certain reluctance on the part of the researchers to ask fundamental questions about the nature of their undertaking—to face up to the prior question on the answer to which much of their work rests—what sort of researches are involved in educational research?[2] For people who undertake what is generically termed 'educational research' can obviously be involved in very different sorts of procedures according to the nature of the questions they ask. Furthermore, they rarely seem, in this country, to investigate the questions that appear to me of most importance—such as that relating to the sub-cultures of youth, the mythologies of adolescence.

But to undertake to educate someone is essentially to be involved in a moral activity; built into the logic of the word is the notion of change to a desired end. And, therefore, questions

[1] Implying, that is, effectiveness in achieving a worthwhile aim. The sinister aspects of efficiency in education are exposed in R. E. Callahan's *Education and the Cult of Efficiency*, which, though concerned with America, is increasingly relevant to the English scene with the growing subordination of education to business interests.

[2] Cf. Chapter 8 below.

of value are always involved. Now, there is a sense in which all education is education for life—the conflict between those who advocate academic learning and those who recommend education for life, in effect, boils down to two different sets of assumptions about the relative value of different sorts of human activity; the man who spends his time investigating the salt trade of the fourteenth century can be at least as much alive as the man who makes a garden shed with his own hands—though there has recently been a fad to regard the latter form of activity as, in some curious way, more 'lived' than the former. Yet, it is in the discussion of aims that much modern educational discourse is at its most distressingly thin. For one thing, prescriptions usually involve large abstractions such as 'citizenship', 'self-development' and the like which have yet to encounter the clarificatory therapy induced by nearly fifty years of linguistic analysis. But, as much to the point, is the frequent poverty of attitude, the lack of density of experience, the qualitative thinness implicit in the specific relationships or acquirements to which these large abstractions refer. I would, indeed, urge that the two writers on education in English in the twentieth century of major importance are D. H. Lawrence and T. S. Eliot; and their work is of importance because they, alone, ask the fundamental questions; in the one case, about the psychic nature and development of the individual, and, in the other, about the nature of our social order; they challenge, that is, the whole trend of events in the twentieth-century world and force from us a justification or modification of our thinking about education which must come to terms with their profounder psychic vision and the greater qualitative richness of the world they inhabit. This world is defined in detail in their literary works; it challenges the facile recommendations of the educational 'establishment' as it manifests itself, too often, in government committee recommendation or academic pronouncement. And yet, my bet is that among professional educators less than 20 per cent will have read Lawrence and not so very many more the *Notes Towards the Definition of Culture*. It is a thousand pities that education, a matter of enormous importance in a world which is going to depend on it more and more, should have produced some of the least educated literature of our times. Part of the responsibility rests with the ordinary university academic, whose almost total indifference in the past to the frighteningly complex and difficult problems of education in a mass society—on the grounds that 'education is what I do' —is now coming home to roost.

In urging the pre-eminence of Eliot and Lawrence, I would not be misunderstood. Although Blake argued that 'The tigers of wrath are wiser than the horses of instruction,' the thoroughbreds among the horses—men of the stature of Dewey, of Mannheim, of Durkheim, of Whitehead have their explicit contribution to make. But they represent, in the discursive nature of their writings and in the assumptions in terms of which they work, the fundamentally positivistic trend of our civilization. The value of Lawrence and Eliot stems from the fact that they have a mode of apprehending the world where the evaluative stress falls somewhat differently; for, of course, their explicit writings on education can only be understood in relation to the imaginative nature of their experience revealed in the poetry and novels. It is this difference of perspective which is vital in the elucidation of that most difficult and complex of moral problems, 'how shall I educate my children?' At bottom, the aim of education must be to help towards a satisfactory life experience at the level of consciousness implicit in the individual child. If this happened, we would have less talk about status and class, less jealous scrutiny of eleven plus, less belief that matters of purely bureaucratic organization can provide us with an adequate educative experience.[1]

[1] I have written on both Lawrence and Eliot at length elsewhere. An essay on D. H. Lawrence appears in *Freedom and Authority in Education* (Faber, 1952); and an essay on Eliot is to appear shortly in an American compilation: *The Ideal of the Educated Man throughout the Ages*.

Education and the Literary Intelligence

I

The disparagement of the rationalistic is a not infrequent manifestation in some current forms of writing; though what is intended by 'rational' is usually left somewhat vague. In so far as my own attitude towards rationalism is equivocal, depending on what more precisely is meant in the particular context by the word, I would like to explain what I do intend by it when I employ it in a derogatory sense, what use of the reason I approve of, and how this links with the 'life' of the emotions—which I think our education should do a good deal more to foster—and with the literary intelligence with which this chapter is explicitly concerned.

The word 'rationalism' is indeed used to refer to a number of quite different ways of employing the reason. In the seventeenth century, for instance, reason was a means to participation in the divine nature, affording access to the intelligible world, the world of essences. In the eighteenth century, it becomes an acquisition rather than an inheritance, a tool, an instrument of thought which, like most tools, needed sharpening. Reason, indeed, 'dissolves everything merely factual, all simple data of experience, and everything believed on the evidence of revelation, tradition and authority; and it does not rest content until it has analyzed all these things into their simplest component parts and into their last elements of belief and opinion' (Cassirer, *The Philosophy of the Enlightenment*, p. 13). From the analysed parts it reconstructs a new whole; its two main functions (and I use the word advisedly, for reason, in this sense, is exercised as a process) are those of 'analytic dissection and synthetic reconstruction' (op. cit., p. 16).

It is the ramifications of this type of mentality that I tend to regard with some measure of mistrust. Such a mind is at once sceptical and arrogant—sceptical because it is brought up to doubt rather than to respect or accept, arrogant because it is visited by few doubts as to the solutions it offers on the basis of a synthetical reconstruction. The rationalist's concern to bring everything to the bar of his judgment implies the assumption that what he there sees is all there is to see; for as his synthesis cannot comprise more than is involved in his analysis, his proferring of solutions to problems—and these his analytic mind smells out with the pertinacity of a bloodhound—involves the implication that the field has been completely covered, all facets considered, in the presentation of the 'solution'. He must always be restless because he is continually concerned with the necessity of rearrangement; and the rearrangement usually involves the ironing out of some complexity which he may regard as wasteful—he is a great enemy of waste, under which heading he is inclined to include aspects of social life which fail to fit in with the narrow range of his morality.

For, of course, in the practice of rationalism as I have noted it, there is a strong morality. Partly this morality is relevant to, is indeed the driving instigator of, the propensity for analysis which is a basic characteristic of this sort of mind. The mind which sees problems is the mind which assumes the moral necessity of solutions; and solutions can carry with them the titivations of the spirit which are stimulated by the delights of interference impowered. As the solutions spring nearly always out of initial simplifications—for analysis always implies abstraction from a totality, a complex—a fine heat is often generated by the resistance encountered from those whose life is thus being oversimplified and who reject the encroaching 'solutions'. Furthermore, as there is usually an emotional basis to the analytic enterprises—part indignation, part assertion—the rationalist is not without a contagious emotionality. He is not, indeed, without feeling; but his feelings are coarsened in that they are usually directed externally to the bare *facts* implicit in the processes of analysis and synthesis rather than employed as partners in the act of discovery; so that the sympathetic consciousness, which could inform the very acts of penetration and reconstruction, becomes simply an external goad to the process, which thus lacks the subtlety that intellect made complex by feeling and feeling refined by intelligence could afford.

Hence the rationalist is very much at the mercy of 'ideas', abstractions. He is not, as I have indicated, without emotions; though, in general, he prides himself on the fact that he keeps them carefully divorced from his reason, for to be swayed by emotion is one of the worst crimes in the rationalist's calendar. He prides himself, indeed, on the 'coldness' of his intellectual prowess, on the detachment from feeling that this implies; though, as so much of human intercourse involves feeling, his boast of being unaffected is some measure of his unfitness to comment on human affairs. But, of course, the affective life will not be denied; and it emerges in simplifications which lead either to sentimentality or to indignation at the spectacle of a human nature which refuses to be cut to rationalist size. Because, in a sense, his emotional life is a by-product of his main concern, the rationalist's feelings tend to be crude and unrefined.[1] Excluded from what he regards as the main business of life, it takes its revenge in subtle falsifications and myopic strivings. The notion of the 'dissociation of sensibility' has recently been under attack because, it is complained, it is not in fact particularly associated with what happened in the seventeenth century; it seems, indeed, always to have been with us. Whether it corresponds historically with that era or not, however, it certainly appears to point to something of significance in the developing consciousness of our own day. For it seems to imply

[1] There is much more of the tradition of French rationalism in Rousseau than is commonly appreciated; for, indeed, the boasted sensibility is little more than a crude sentimentality. An essay on Rousseau which will substantiate this fact appears later in the book.

this split between the force of the intelligence, manifested in 'ideas', and of the emotions, manifested in the vitality of living. That conception of the 'unified sensibility', which so many of the great modern writers have attempted to reassert, whether it represents an historical reality or an artifact in the minds of moderns aware of a 'much-divided civilization', nevertheless serves to indicate a closeness of relationship between the intellectual and the affective life which is quite foreign to the rationalist.

Other characteristics of the rationalist are his concern for perfection and his tendency to eschew variety. These characteristics in part spring from that tendency to abstraction we have already indicated; for to abstract is to choose out what seems essential; and what seems essential relates to that which is free from the vagaries of time and place. This almost inevitably accompanies his habit of thinking in terms of problems and of the scale on which problems become significant. For his most characteristic sort of problem is that which concerns itself with categories—categories of people or actions. Thus the local conflict of two people with different coloured skins becomes 'the colour problem'; and the repercussions of a little juvenile misbehaviour becomes 'the delinquency problem'. Individuals, indeed, become subsumed under general categories—an offshoot, perhaps, of that movement of thought in the scientific field, which attempts to find explanations in terms of greater and greater generality and whose characteristic thought movement has so profoundly affected the whole rationalist outlook.

In the place of this rationalist outlook, I would certainly not wish to press the merits of an undisciplined intuitionism, a rabid emotionalism or a trusting to any rampant form of irrationalism; I do not want to eschew the use of the reason: only to refine it. In speaking of the affective life, for instance, I would stress the necessity for the disciplining or 'ordering' of the emotions; and this disciplining can only be carried out by forces which, in the shorthand into which we are inevitably forced by the poverty of our vocabulary and of our understandings on this score, to describe as intellectual. But this is not a simple matter of keeping a rein on the passions—for such is the rationalist's solution. It is rather a matter of harnessing the emotions to the service of the intellect—or if that is too crude a way of expressing the subtly interpenetrating nature of the relationship between the two, then it is necessary to insist that just as the emotions are controlled by the intellect, so the intellect needs to be refined by what of feeling can afford it depth and concreteness; so that one comes to agree with George Eliot when she asserted her realization that 'speculative truth begins to appear but a shadow of individual minds'. Such a mind, then, will not fail to analyse or to synthesize; but its analysis will bear in mind what Mill had to say of Bentham: 'Nobody's synthesis can be more complete than his analysis. If in his survey of human nature and life he has left any element out, then, wheresoever that element exerts any influence, his conclusions will fail, more or less, in their application.' It is, it seems to me, this close conjunction of intellect and feeling which issues in that imaginative insight which is our most profitable way of thinking about human 'sciences' (of which education must always, in certain of its guises, be one of the most important) and which it is peculiarly the function of literature to help to train.[1]

Challenged to produce an example of that combination of reason and the imagination, that ability to feel into situations which does not eschew analysis, I could cite Sir Winston Churchill's famous memorandum on the rebuilding of the blitzed House of Commons:

'Its shape should be oblong and not semi-circular. Here is a very potent factor in our political life. The semi-circular assembly which appeals to political theorists, enables every individual or every group to move round the centre, adopting various shades of pink according as the weather changes. . . . It is easy for an individual to move through these insensible

[1] Cf. H. Stuart Hughes, *Consciousness and Society*. Professor Hughes, in characterizing the period 1890–1930 with which he is concerned in his book, writes that many thinkers during this period came to see that 'Man as an actor in society . . . was seldom decisively influenced by logical considerations: supra- or infra-rational values of one sort or another usually guided his conduct.'

gradations from Left to Right, but the act of crossing the Floor is one which requires serious consideration. I am well informed on this matter, for I have accomplished that difficult process, not only once, but twice. . . .

'It should not be big enough to contain all its members at once without overcrowding, and there should be no question of every member having a separate seat reserved for him. . . . If the House is big enough to contain all its Members nine-tenths of its debates will be conducted in the depressing atmosphere of an almost empty or half-empty chamber. The essence of good House of Commons speaking is the conversational style, the facility for quick informal interruptions and interchanges. Harangues from a rostrum would be a bad substitute. . . . But the conversational style requires a fairly small space, and there should be on great occasions a sense of crowd and urgency. There should be a sense . . . that great matters are being decided, there and then, by the House.

This seems to me to illustrate, at its level, the working of the 'feeling intellect' in the yet eminently practical affairs of life. (One can see what a pure rationalist might have made of the situation.) For Churchill shows that what, on the surface, appears perfectly 'reasonable'—space in relation to numbers—takes no cognizance of what is implicit in the developed life of an institution, which involves the 'feel' of the occasions for which it is constituted as well as their rationally assessable circumstances.

The people who have demonstrated this particular sort of intelligence most fully have been the literary artists—those who, in George Eliot's terms, possess a 'soul in which knowledge passes instantaneously into feeling, and feeling flashes back in a new organ of knowledge.' The relevance of such writers to our thinking about education, then, I wish to consider.

II

It is always dangerous to set up one discipline as a substitute for another or to think that a training in one field necessarily enables one to make essential discriminations in another. Cardinal Newman wisely pleaded that fields of study should learn to keep their bounds, and should not presume to invade areas in which their nature did not enable them to judge fruitfully.

At the same time, it is my contention that the literary intelligence is of such a kind that its relevance stretches further than to the criticism of new books or the professing of *belles-lettres*, activities to which Frederic Harrison, whom Matthew Arnold took to task, would have confined the man of culture, in the predominantly literary significance of the title. For the literary artist, if his concern is truly, as I believe it to be, with life, necessarily encompasses a number of fields in a way which may not completely recommend itself to those who have concerned themselves with the logical and abstract development of those disciplines but which may, nevertheless, reveal useful awareness and illuminating insights. He is concerned with life as a process —'living'—and those human activities which imply both a practical and a theoretical aspect, such as politics, sociology and social psychology, ethics and education, can learn something from his appreciation of the need for discrimination within process and activity which forms an essential element of his art.

But, first, what is implied by 'literary intelligence', intelligence, that is to say, trained in relation to that enlargement of the sensibilities which good literature involves? To begin with, it denotes an appreciation of certain of the resources of language which literary works tend to use in a particular way. A relevant distinction between the specifically literary use of language and its use in other contexts has been admirably expressed by Dr. Leavis. 'Philosophy, we say, is "abstract" and poetry "concrete". Words in poetry invite us, not to "think about" and judge but to "feel into" or "become"—to realize a complex experience that is given in words.' Thus we partake of literary experience in a way in which it would be untrue to say that we partake of the abstractions of the political philosopher or the social scientist. The literary artist, to a degree, *engages* us in his experience through his handling of language, through metaphor and rhythm, in order to bring into play a full and delicate perceptiveness, engaging both the intelligence and the emotions—the 'feeling intellect'

Consider the handling of the political theme in Conrad's *The Secret Agent.* It will be readily conceded that there is perhaps more to be said for revolutionary political activity than Conrad finds to say in that novel. Nevertheless, we appreciate that Conrad's perceptiveness provides us with insights into the life of politics relevant, in some measure, to such political activity, though the political theorist notes them too little. Thus, Conrad explores the relationship between abstract belief and individual temperament, temperament subjected to a particular set of pressures which arise from its concrete relationships with the world around it. We see a terrorist outrage reduced through the irony of circumstances to the level of tragi-comedy; and the effect is created not by telling us *about* the incident, but by a subtle direction of our focus of attention through irony displayed in a particular mode of handling language, a mode which employs coolness and objectivity together with a measure of the sardonic—as in the description: 'Mr. Verloc, steady like a rock—a soft kind of rock.'[1]

The effect is that we achieve a wholeness of conception, an embedded quality of idea in temperament and circumstance which we find nearer to the actual behaviour of human beings in political circumstances than we would guess at from the writings of political theorists. We see that 'idea', as associated with the individual, is but an element in a complex of personal ambitions and egotistic self-projections; and we note that decisions come to be made as a result of a combination of overt political allegiance with unassessable private motives and hidden desires.

Now the greatest writers are concerned with more than experience *tout court*; as I have noted, they make discriminations among experiences. There is an evaluative aspect which comes to wear very much the appearance of a moral concern. I do not mean that the novelist or dramatist is concerned to preach. I

[1] I have developed this theme more fully in an essay on 'Conrad and Politics' which appeared in *E.L.H.*, June 1958.

mean that the writer's disposition of his incidents, the effects which he allows to emerge from the interplay of character, the particular way in which he resolves his drama inevitably bear witness to his set of values and to his appreciation of the differences to be marked between varying courses of action. In so far as the dramatic writer and the novelist are inevitably involved in the clashes arising from human inter-relationship and in the choices which have to be made in human behaviour, their account can hardly remain ethically neutral. This does not necessarily imply anything so crude as good triumphing over vanquished bad, of course. But it does mean that our sympathies have been actively engaged or repelled, in terms of concrete particularities of behaviour by which we have been led to discriminate between the different values of various types of conduct. A great deal of the work of Henry James, as I have argued elsewhere,[1] is concerned to define the conditions of moral restraint in a social order which, due in part to the breakdown of traditional sanctions, offered opportunities for undiscriminating 'experience' largely as opportunities for egotistic exploitation. *Roderick Hudson* affords a good example of James's treatment of the theme. Behind James's concern lies the summing-up of Hilary St. George, the Master: 'I've had everything. In other words, I've missed everything.' Moral sensibility necessitates other conditions for fruition; and restraint, to the point at least that it does not become an excoriating renunciation, forms an essential element of moral freedom.

At the same time, the writer is essentially concerned with the 'new', the freshly apprehended. As in his handling of words he is the enemy of the cliché, save for the express purpose of irony, so in relationship and incident he is the foe of the habitual or the conventional. He explores beneath the surface of appearances to the realities beneath. Hence the force of Lawrence's assertion that the novel 'can inform and lead into new places the flow of our sympathetic consciousness, and it can lead our sympathy away in recoil from things gone dead.' Against the inertia of

[1] Cf. 'Morals and Civilisation in Henry James', *Cambridge Journal*, December 1953.

custom and habit the writer urges the life of individual consciousness with its unique vision; and even when he reasserts tradition, as in the case of T. S. Eliot, it is tradition revivified and evolving, a genuine re-creation in the individual consciousness: 'Tradition cannot mean standing still.' In this way, uniqueness *in continuity* is assured. For, however much the decay of the European tradition has involved the isolation of the writer, he is always aware of the need for rootedness. Isolation is not enough, sheer self-assertion a false way out. 'Thank God I am not free, any more than a rooted tree is free,' was Lawrence's cry. If then, the writer finds himself a stranger in the house, his strangeness is not that of the casual visitor but arises from the strain of belonging:

> *Home is where one starts from. As we grow older*
> *The world becomes stranger, the pattern more complicated*
> *Of dead and living. Not the intense moment*
> *Isolated, with no before and after,*
> *But a lifetime burning in every moment*
> *And not the lifetime of one man only*
> *But of old stones that cannot be deciphered.*

And so, as literature shows, there is the world of personal experience and that of traditional social experience; yet the latter, even at its finest, is never adequate, in itself, at any level, to the former, though it remains an essential datum in personal development. Often there seems to exist a dichotomy between the 'appearance' as it manifests itself in the individual consciousness and the 'reality', as it seems, of the social circumstance, so that there is tension between the desire and the fulfilment, between the dream and the awakening. But such an antithesis of individual and society expresses too sharp a division, as if it were the integration into social circumstance one should seek, shedding the dream in the awakening and dismissing the desire in the paucity of fulfilment. Whereas, in Conrad's *Lord Jim*, we are exhorted to 'follow the dream, and again to follow the dream —and so—*ewig—usque ad finem*'. For social circumstance is both a datum to, and a creation of, the individual; thus, when the stranger-poet enters the house, he encounters the brick he himself has laid, enters the room he has himself inhabited. Tragedy involves this reciprocity: 'O, I have ta'en too little care of this,' cries Lear on the heath, driven out by his own blindness as much as by his 'pelican daughters'. 'In my end is my beginning.'

But, what has all this to do with education? Even allowing that a training of the literary intelligence involves the perception of some of these things, what possible relevance have they to the work of the classroom or the lecture-room?

III

An increasingly common cry of the educationist has been that it is his function to teach his pupils how to live. 'Life is the trade I would teach him,' urged Rousseau; 'to prepare us for complete living is the function which education has to discharge,' said Herbert Spencer. Dewey and Susan Isaacs say much the same thing. Now, once this relationship between school and life has been thus so strongly asserted—and, after all, it provokes a measure of agreement—it is relevant to enquire into the conceptions of life which lie behind this assertion of aim. What necessitate discussion are qualitative considerations relevant to the nature of the human existence aimed at.

In so far as these educationists reveal a common spirit—and among writers who display considerable differences, their agreement must not be urged too far—they concur in accepting the main tendencies of the civilization of their day; this is, paradoxically, true even of Rousseau, despite the apparent contradictoriness of his opinions and his indignation against the society of his time. For they all agree in regarding education, in some measure, as a means to gaining control over the environment, as a development of the assertive will. They are all deeply imbued with the scientific spirit—though their science is technological rather than descriptive. Thus they accept, fundamentally, the general movement of their civilization, which is towards the implementation of the Baconian thesis: 'Knowledge is power'; they no longer regard knowledge as a means to aesthetic enjoyment, but as an aid to secular control. Impressed with little sense of the mystery of things or with scepticism arising from self-doubt, their virtues are the Robinson Crusoe virtues of self-help and prudential management, except that in the main they no longer count God as a factor to contend with or to propitiate into active alliance by repentance and Bible-reading. Yet we remember it was a literary intelligence which proclaimed Bacon's essays as 'Good advice for Satan's kingdom.' It was another literary intelligence which diagnosed a major effect of the study of science: 'One would think that it might materialize people . . . but in fact they seem to end in conceiving only of a world of formulas. . . .' It is the literary intelligence of T. S. Eliot which deprecates our 'age of bustle, programmes, platforms, scientific progress, humanitarianism and revolutions which improved nothing'. D. H. Lawrence makes some fundamental criticisms of modern life in *Fantasia of the Unconscious*, which remains at once one of the most penetrating analyses of 'this strange disease of modern life', and the major educational textbook of our day; it persuades that our precarious complacencies form but a thin surface over the abyss.

What I am intending by these few evocative examples is that the educationist needs the profoundest penetration possible into the nature of human existence before his claim to educate 'for life' can be accepted as valid. For, at a time when we are urged so strongly to afford 'experience' at all levels of educational endeavour, the qualitative considerations we take into account when deciding what constitutes relevant and *valuable* experience are of paramount importance. And here, I would contend that the literary intelligence penetrates more deeply than does the educationist; read side by side, it is the literary work that reveals the skull beneath the skin, glimpses the 'horror and the glory', we note, not the educational. Even where method is concerned, the writer, because like Conrad he has wrestled with the Lord for his creation, has much to contribute; thus the attempt, characteristic of 'progressive' theory, to throw the onus of responsibility on to the pupil, as if our aim were merely to follow his spontaneous interests, or to allow to evolve what is immanent in his nature by a passive attending, obscures that tension between mind and external world which the literary intelligence has found a peculiarly fruitful source of creation. Genuine creativity, Arnold thought, involved both the man and the moment; it lay in the 'faculty' of being happily inspired by a certain intellectual and spiritual atmosphere, by a certain order of ideas, when it finds itself in them'. If, in the adult world, these conditions are difficult to fulfil, there is no reason why, where more immature minds are concerned, scholastic institutions should not make a conscious effort to provide them, if only the teacher will appreciate the positive nature of his function. But to be able to do this means not only the courage of one's convictions; it implies also a trained sensibility capable of making essential discriminations among varieties of experience, of seeing the function of the experience in relation to the stage of development of the pupil, of being able, that is, to make relevant choices. Thus, we need to make the distinction Arnold made in his school reports, between what studies can be considered as 'formative' and what cannot. Moreover, we need to make relevant distinctions as to what features of the life around the pupil should be encouraged to exert their influences and what should be combated in the only place where they are likely to be combated, the scholastic institution. If the philosophy of education has some relation to moral philosophy, then our attempt to frame an adequate syllabus needs the moral leavening the literary artist can afford us. One of Arnold's most important indications of the value of the literary intelligence is seen in the concrete judgments he pronounced on the quality of mid-Victorian civilization in *Culture and Anarchy*. His appreciation of the need for the best that had been thought and said led him to a social analysis of the decline in the cultural standards of his time which, in our age of the cinema, the comic strip, commercial television, mass-production and ribbon development has an even greater relevance than when it was first written. All these cultural manifestations imply an appeal to our perceptions and sensibilities. In so far as they nurture—as it must be admitted on the most elementary analysis, that they do nurture—the imaginative life, they must imply some degradation (to push it no further) of our perceptive faculties; faculties engaged, that is, in human relationships and in the insights relevant to such relationships. They thus necessarily lead to a coarsening of the sensibilities and, in consequence, of the social fabric.

In other words, what is necessary is a sense of adequate standards in a variety of fields and of the relevance of those standards to the educative process. The aim is not, be it noted, the formation of dilettante tastes or the creation of a 'private heaven for aesthetes', but that some improvement may be made in the coarser sensibilities of the age to better the qualities of human responsiveness and human insight and this at a variety of levels, each with its own integrity.

The notion of the need to reassert standards inevitably raises the question of the part played by Dr. Leavis and *Scrutiny* in the process in recent years.[1] Even if the need to reassert standards be admitted, was the astringency of *Scrutiny* a desirable feature or did it not militate, by its intransigency, against the object which it had in view? One can at least understand, even if one cannot sympathize with, some such questioning. Granted, that is, that the literary intelligence—and *Scrutiny* was a predominantly literary organ, devoted to the refining of the literary and critical intelligence—has this function to perform in defining the qualities of living, would not a more persuasive manner have aroused less hostility and been more effective?

Less hostility, perhaps; but, more effective—I do not think so. For in a world so given over to the socio-personal affinities—they stretch beyond the literary world—the only refuge has lain in an unremitting personal integrity, to see the object as, in itself, it really is (I quote Arnold again) and to state what one sees with the maximum cogency and forcefulness. Rarely before in our civilization can such an effort of repudiation have been necessary or has the effort to see the object as in itself it really is been attended with such gargantuan difficulties. Yet increased ability to discriminate cuts both ways; it may increase sensiti-

[1] The whole of *Scrutiny* has, of course, just been republished by the C.U.P.

vity to the desirable positive, but it also clarifies the view of the undesirable negative. And the realization that what is negative represents so much that is powerful in the life of today, so much that is socially entrenched and that, being socially entrenched, has immense influence and power for interference, implies that it can only be met by an unyielding obstinacy and a resolute vigilance. 'If thy hand offend thee, cut it off.' Sensitivity does not necessitate softness, for discrimination which serves only to excuse is no discrimination but palliation. It is not possible to serve two masters; and the temptations—social, material, financial—of the social-personal 'game' are too essentially there to permit dallying or flirtation, even in the name of 'good personal relationships'. For, if there are personal considerations, there are impersonal ones, too; and the impersonal ones, achieved with integrity and resolution, reflect back on the personal, refining and purifying. There, if anywhere, must be found the excuse—motivation, I would rather say—for astringency supported by analytic evidence, such as *Scrutiny* provided; and, in consequence, for the way in which one conceives the school, in certain of its functions, and at the appropriate levels, as something that repudiates aspects of our current society.

The literary intelligence, then, intensely aware of its present plight, impresses on us the need for discrimination as the necessary precursor to the creation of a vital and living climate of opinion in which intelligent life can be sustained and creative abilities released; and creative abilities, be it remembered, need the astringent and the right kind of discrimination, implying renunciation, for their proper flourishing.[1] At the same time, such discrimination can inhibit that tendency to abstraction which characterizes the formulation of educational ideas. For literary activity is perpetually concerned with particularities and concrete cases, as I have indicated. We remember George Eliot's strictures on Mr. Stelling's 'regimen for all minds', which turned out so uncomfortably for Tom Tulliver, and her

[1] This should be borne constantly in mind, in all discussion below on the education of the affective life—the 'very culture of the feelings' which proceeds as a matter of refinement and cultivation.

analyses of the metaphors of ploughing and harrowing which guided Mr. Stelling's apprehensions of his educational aims.

But, on this further issue of the unsuitability of Tom Tulliver's education to his nature, surely, it may be urged, this is to-day *vieux jeu?* Has not a great deal of printed and lecture space been devoted precisely to the question of individual differences, and have not the psychologists for ages past been urging the need for a careful assessment of the age, aptitude and abilities of the individual child? It is true we have got beyond Mr. Stelling; but we are hardly yet ready to dispense with the insights the literary intelligence can afford us. For one thing, though the psychologist can tell us a good many facts about child nature and the learning process which we did not know so clearly before, he can give us no guidance on how we are to make use of these facts or on the relative value we assign to one set of facts as opposed to another. The psychologist's findings are couched in the form: 'If you do so and so, then such and such is likely to happen'; but such a statement does not decide for us whether 'such and such' is to be regarded as good or bad. It is logically impermissible to derive a judgment of value from a statement of fact. In actual practice, however, we do note the tendency of the psychologist to urge concepts implying desirable behaviour in some such terms as 'mental health', 'social adjustment' and the like. And the meek acceptance by the educational world of these concepts is matter for some disquiet. Even some slight acquaintance with literature would be sufficient to convince that 'social adjustment' is a concept which needs to be handled with the greatest care. Many novels of the first rank take as part of their major concern an analysis of what is implied by such a concept. I need only mention parts of Henry James's *The Portrait of a Lady* and L. H. Myers's *The Root and the Flower* to make plain a characteristic feature of many modern writings. Yet most psychologists show little of that subtlety of penetration, displayed in these novels in concrete instances of incident and character, which marks these writers. It has needed the highly trained literary sensibility of Professor D. W. Harding, distinguished as much in the capacity of literary critic as of psychologist, to demonstrate some of the dangers attendant on too uncritical an acceptance of the 'social adjustment' formula. 'So much has been heard in psychology of the need for the individual to "adjust" himself to his society that we may sometimes forget that social groups can in turn be assessed for their adequacy to their own members,' he points out in his book *Social Psychology and Individual Values*; and it is interesting to note that, in defining the relation of the individual to society, he draws on numerous examples from literature.

But, it will be urged, even if this is allowed, surely one must admit the psychologist's success in drawing attention to the need for the consideration of individual difference. Of course, it would be idle to deny that the psychologist's research does in fact reveal a variety of individual difference which has been accepted as a primary datum in the work of education. But the precise importance of this emphasis on individual difference, the degree to which it sensitizes the mind to the nature of the differences and their relevance in educational situations are matters where the literary intelligence has at least as much, if not more, to contribute, than the psychologist. For the psychologist, to the extent to which he considers himself a scientist, to the extent to which, that is to say, he does not employ a sort of intuition which is analogous to that of the literary artist (so that Freud could say that he was only establishing on a scientific basis notions that the writer had appreciated for centuries), is inevitably involved in the acceptance of psychological fact at a certain level only. To be of use to the scientist-psychologist, for the framing of hypotheses concerning human behaviour, the deployment of psychological fact necessitates the isolation of that fact from the complex of mental life which it at once expresses and is an expression of. Now, a psychological fact to the literary mind is significant only to the degree to which it exemplifies ('grows out of' would specify the organic nature of the relationship more adequately) a more complex state of mind or disposition of the personality.

In other words, the 'fact' is seen in a network of affiliations which both help to produce it and are produced by it. Thus the overt manifestations of jealousy in Othello are seen in relation to a particular self-regarding aspect of the personality, achieve a close correlation with that pride of place and personal dignity so admirably conveyed in the opening scenes of the play, and which have their excellent side. The psychologist's attempt to 'explain' such a jealousy on the grounds of insecurity induced by some phenomenon such as colour-bar prejudice may have its 'therapeutic' point; though it is relevant to mention that such an explanation is never a complete one, but demands a particular potentiality of the personality in relation to a particular hostility of the white races. The point is, however, that Shakespeare imposes on us through the subtlety of the verse rhythms used in Othello's later speeches the special quality of self-deception and unreality which marks the development of his jealousy (cf. the hieratic movement of the opening of the speech beginning: 'It is the cause, it is the cause my soul,' together with the later intensity of sensuous suggestion); and this provides a mode of apprehending the state of Othello's mind and, by implication, minds under similar circumstances, which enables us—employing Dr. Leavis's phrase noted above—to 'feel into' the situation in a way beyond the scope of the psychologist. In other words, the literary artist enables us to achieve a degree of imaginative projection which is of the greatest usefulness in any concrete situation, particularly the educational.

Then again, the analysis briefly noted above of Conrad has implications for the educationist. For, just as political 'views' need to be seen in the full complex of the personality which holds them, so we need to have the same apprehension concerning educational views. Notions on the desirability of certain changes; the stubborn association of a particular viewpoint with the prestige of the ego, our relative unwillingness to submit our stock notions to the 'free play of mind' (Arnold's phrase again) all tend to inhibit that creation of a 'current of true and fresh ideas,' which are of the utmost relevance in the developing process of framing an educational system. I have noticed that there is the blindness and the unwillingness to examine assumption of the 'progressive' as well as of the traditionalist, of the exponent of the comprehensive school as well as of the defender of the grammar school. But it is of the essence of the literary intelligence that it encourages 'impersonality', a measure of detachment from the pressure of personal and too often egotistic opinion, a willingness to see round and about, an acceptance at times of 'negative capability'; and this because it is aware that the life of situations is complex and not subject to the application of a formula, that truth is partial in the individual, and that flexibility of outlook is the only refuge in the war between entrenched opinions, such as the educational world currently displays.

But, nevertheless, there *are* decisions to be made, action to be taken. It is part of the difficulties of our time that action is so often too little aware of the complexities involved; changes come to be mooted on purely 'rational' grounds which take too little note of what lies outside the purview of abstract reason but which is yet immensely powerful in human affairs; so that the results too often mock at the rationalist's efforts at 'improvement'. We note this currently in the emphasis on organization which marks our thinking about secondary education. (It is typical of the rationalist, of course, to put his faith in organization as such.) The sort of education implicit in the common curriculum recommended for the comprehensive school indicates the power of rationalistic, abstract notions to prevent our thinking about the real capacities of children; so that, as T. S. Eliot has pointed out in *Notes towards the Definition of Culture*, the sort of education we impose on our people today is an abstraction remote from the real pressures of living. For, behind the comprehensive philosophy lies a muddle of egalitarian and meritocratic implications, largely of political origin, which blind us to the natures of children in front of us. Such implications spring, indeed, from a quite inadequate notion of what constitutes opportunity. To learn the lesson of Tom Tulliver is to repudiate both the watered down grammar school and the extended vocational syllabus[1] which is what, in general, the

[1] Because, of course, most of such children have no work to do of a sort which demands more than a few days' training on the shop floor. Cf. my *Education in an Industrial Society*, *passim*.

comprehensive school has produced for the less able. It is to be encouraged to probe beneath the abstractions and generalities in terms of which so much educational debate is conducted to the living core of the children we teach.

When we do this, we see that the problem is basically cultural, not political. A culture provides the means to self-identification which characterizes a people; it provides the terms in which a people thinks and feels. The disintegration of accepted social forms which has followed on industrialization has posed the question of personal identity with a peculiar poignancy in the midst of today's social fluidities. One of the major themes of modern literature—it goes back at least to Stendhal's *Le Rouge et le Noir*—lies in the search for an answer to the question 'Who am I?'. Surely it is just such a question that, in relation to the children he is educating, faces the educationist. What he sees is that our society, through its mass culture, provides a number of substitute answers to this question as compensation for the boredom and emptiness of much industrial work and as a means to commercial exploitation. It is because he defines identity at a more profound and satisfying level that the literary artist has so much to offer, in this and in the other ways I have tried to define.

1955

'Emile' Reconsidered

What is often referred to as the 'progressive movement' invokes, like most conceptions of education, theories both of knowledge and of human nature. The theory of knowledge appears recognizably in the work of Bacon, though the slant of mind which helped to induce Bacon's epistemology had appeared some time before. The view of man's nature begins to be effective with the romantic reaction against the Enlightenment, towards the middle of the eighteenth century; it, too, contains elements taken from an earlier movement of opinion. A key figure in this reaction was Rousseau; and as the author of a historically significant book concerned with education his conception of man has had an important place in the rise of 'progressive' ideas.

Notoriously, Rousseau's ideas display many inconsistencies, and it is not unknown to discover contradictions in successive paragraphs. What he has to say about his musical compositions applies to his work in general: 'It is true that my work, uneven and irregular, was sometimes sublime and sometimes insipid, as must be the work of everyone who only elevates himself by flashes of genius, without the support of scientific training'[1] (*Confessions*, i, p. 306). He presents, then, a series of insights rather than a logically coherent system; he is, in *Emile*, nearer the artist than the technical philosopher.[2] Indeed, his educa-

[1] The references are to the Everyman edition of the *Confessions*.

[2] In the *Contrat Social*, however, he supplies a much greater degree of logical coherence. And, even in *Emile*, a number of the recommendations

tional recommendations often deprecate what only systematic training and application can provide. In assessing someone who depends much on 'sensibility', indeed consciously evokes it as a standard of reference, we need to define the particular nature of that sensibility. It is essential, therefore, to approach *Emile* through the *Confessions*.[1] This is more necessary as one of the latest and most comprehensive of the French commentators considers it possible that *Emile* is neither 'un roman tissu d'impossibles rêves, ni un traité dogmatique de pédagogie, ni un faisceau d'intuitions sur l'enfant: il est une Rêverie au sens roussien du mot, c'est-à-dire Pensée et Vie. . . . Il l'a écrit comme un chapitre essentiel, définitif, de sa philosophie de l'Homme.'[2] There is a close connection between the 'Rêverie' of *Emile* and certain manifestations of Jean Jacques's inner life; though to dismiss *Emile* as a dream would be to ignore its curious appearance of logicality, its pervasive emphasis on a certain mode of experience which have deceived others than Thomas Day into the possibility of concrete implementation. Certainly, *Emile* has had its effects on practical policies; its observations and insights, its indulgences and sentimentalities have taken their place among our contemporary educational precepts. And the influence of a book is to be measured as much in the terms in which people come to accept it as in the original purposes of the author, even when the latter can be defined with any certainty.

Two things of great importance emerge from a consideration of the *Confessions*: the particular nature of Rousseau's imaginative life, and his quite extraordinary lack, at the profounder levels, of self-knowledge. The impetus of the whole work, indeed, is a self-protectiveness which all too frequently merges into self-righteousness; and certain characteristics of the undertaking and of the terms in which it is conceived raise initial doubts as

follow quite logically from the particular insight on which they are based; as I have noted earlier (p. 35) he is much more in the French rationalist tradition than is commonly accepted.

[1] 'Je ne cherche en Rousseau que l'expression de la sensibilité.'—P. Trahard, *Les Maîtres de la Sensibilité Française au XVIIIe Siècle*. Cf., too, Bertrand Russell, *History of Western Philosophy*, Chapter XIX.

[2] A. Ravier, *L'Education de l'Homme Nouveau*, Vol. II, p. 497.

to the writer's perceptiveness and capacity for detachment. If, as Rousseau contends: 'The real object of my *Confessions* is, to contribute to an accurate knowledge of my inner being in all the different situations of my life' (*Confessions*, i, p. 252), he contributed to this understanding in ways of which he himself had little awareness.[1]

Rousseau early gives the vital clue to the quality of his imaginative life. 'I felt before I thought,' he asserts; much of the 'feeling' came from the fantasy life which, in his very early years was induced by the reading of 'romances': 'In a short time I acquired . . . not only extreme facility in reading and understanding what I read, but a knowledge of the passions that was unique in a child of my age. I had no idea of things in themselves, although all the feelings of actual life were already known to me. I had conceived nothing, but felt everything. These confused emotions which I felt one after the other, certainly did not warp the reasoning powers which I did not as yet possess; but they shaped them in me of a peculiar stamp, and gave me odd and romantic notions of human life, of which experience and reflection have never been able wholly to cure me' (*Confessions*, i, p. 4). Such a tendency to live in terms of fantasy lasted with him throughout his life, as is proved in numerous instances; he even excuses his propensity on the grounds of his own superior virtue: he speaks of 'a too affectionate, too loving and too tender heart, which, being unable to find any in existence resembling it, is obliged to nourish itself with fancies.' His account of his life on the island of St. Pierre, where he retired for a time several years after the publication of *Emile*, indicates its persistence: 'I love to . . . spend the day in trifling without order and sequence, and, in everything, to follow nothing but the caprice of the moment. . . . Frequently, leaving my boat at the mercy of the wind and water, I aban-

[1] Cf. Joseph Conrad: '. . . confessions, a form of literary activity discredited by Jean Jacques Rousseau on account of the extreme thoroughness he brought to the work of justifying his own existence; for that such was his purpose is palpably, even grossly, visible to an unprejudiced eye.' (*A Personal Record.*)

doned myself to aimless reveries, which, although foolish, were none the less delightful' (*Confessions*, ii, pp. 279–82).

Rousseau's famous capacity for 'feeling', then, manifests itself as one of its most characteristic phases, in an abandonment of the normal adult attempts to cope with the world in which we live: 'The idleness that I love is not that of an idler who remains with folded arms in a state of total inactivity, no more thinking than acting. That which I love is that combined idleness of a child who is incessantly in motion without ever doing anything, and that of a dotard, who wanders from one thing to another while his arms are still' (*Confessions*, ii, p. 279). His expression of his awareness of what he was doing should not deceive us into thinking that it betokened any more than a typical example of Rousseauesque self-complacency. He does not expound in order to criticize himself. His reveries, indeed, are of a peculiarly indulgent type; they involve a self-absorption which implies that his emotions are directed only upon himself. There is no out-flowing to the particular situation or person with whom he is in contact, no real admission of the other than self, as there is, for instance, in a writer who betrays certain similarities of assumption, D. H. Lawrence; Rousseau, unlike Lawrence, failed to come to any real understanding of his environment. And this affects the nature of his writing. Whereas one of Lawrence's main virtues lies in his capacity for receptivity, in his imaginative ability to accept and convey the 'spirit of place'—whether it be industrial England, New Mexico, Mediterranean seaboard or Australian bush—one is struck by the justice of Conrad's summing-up of Rousseau: 'He had no imagination, as the most casual perusal of *Emile* will prove.'[1] Rousseau was too absorbed in self to achieve 'impersonality'. (I use the word in the sense defined by T. S. Eliot.) His capacity for observation is gravely limited by the bounds of what he wanted to observe, either as self-justification or compensation. No one more lacks 'negative capability'.[2]

[1] *A Personal Record.*

[2] Rousseau provides, to my mind, an admirable example of Lawrence's 'idealization', 'living from the head' (cf. *Fantasia of the Unconscious*) living,

There is an extremely revealing passage which points out: 'My obstinate nature is unable to bow to facts. It cannot beautify, it must create. Realities appear to it nothing more than they are; it can only embellish the objects of imagination' (*Confessions*, i, p. 156). Here, I believe, is the reason for the peculiar combination of literalness and reverie in *Emile*. There is a fundamental split between 'real life', which Rousseau tends to equate with 'facts' of a technical or scientific nature and 'imagination' which, in effect, involves little more than 'fantasy'. Rousseau has no capacity to 'imagine', in Coleridge's significance of the term: 'it dissolves, diffuses, dissipates, in order to recreate; or when this process is rendered impossible, yet still at all events it struggles to idealize and to unify. It is essentially *vital*, even as all objects (*as* objects) are essentially fixed and dead.'[1] Rousseau never vitalizes. Objects remain dead. Hence there is no 'coalescence of subject and object' in his work, no penetrating perception of 'objects' by the 'vital' self, but two separate worlds—that of self giving rein to sentimental fantasies and expressions of uncontrolled feeling, which he boosted as 'intuition', and that of the outside world, analysed and controlled as he conceives his own *Emile* learning to do, which emerged from his sensational philosophy. This split in the nature of Rousseau's experience lies at the heart of one's dissatisfaction with *Emile*. It mars both his conception of the potentialities of human nature and unduly restricts his purview of the range of human experience. Though Rousseau was aware of the egotism of *amour-propre*, which he was acute enough to

that is to say, in terms of certain mental conceptions of things instead of by direct, intuitive response to unique situations. There are certain likenesses between the two men—their dependence on their own 'sensibilities', for instance, which have been noted before (cf. Jane Soames, 'The Modern Rousseau', in *Life and Letters*, December 1932, an article which otherwise seems to me to misinterpret profoundly the natures of the two men); they provide an interesting comment one on the other, and they are divided, it seems to me, by Lawrence's infinitely greater self-awareness, a self-awareness which despite all the notorious 'difficulty' of the man, induced a certain repose and acceptance, a transcendence of self, which emerges, for instance, in the later letters and in the best novels.

[1] *Biographia Literaria*, Chapter XIII.

note behind the masks which men assumed in society, largely because he himself was particularly affected by certain social disabilities, he was blind to the equally invalidating egotism of self-contemplation which was his own peculiar vice.[1]

Rousseau's vaunted 'sensibility', then, comes to appear a different thing from what it is frequently made out to be; and, indeed, in the all too easy dichotomy which Rousseau made between man and society, one detects an analysis blunted by a particular incapacity for self-understanding. To follow the 'inner light' ('the most untrustworthy and deceitful guide that ever offered itself to wandering humanity,' as T. S. Eliot has called it) with any hope of success requires a self-honesty, an ability to learn from experience and to face the deeper implications of the self which Rousseau nowhere displays. Hence his insistence in the *Confessions* on solitude and individual independence, as against the claims of society, needs to be validated by a profounder understanding of the implications of both the individual and society and of their interactions and interdependences than Rousseau's analysis there reveals. What springs all too frequently from a purely personal antipathy, actuated by personal shyness[2] and a sometimes justifiable sense of boredom, never achieves the dignity of 'impersonal' analysis;[3] so that, in throwing over social constraints, both the idle

[1] His self-justification over the putting away of his children provides a good example of his extraordinary self-righteousness: '. . . is it possible that my warm-heartedness, lively sensibility, readiness to form attachments, the powerful hold which they exercise over me, the cruel heart-breakings I experience when forced to break them off, my natural goodwill towards all my fellow-creatures, my ardent love of the great, the true, the beautiful, and the just; my horror of evil of every kind, my utter inability to hate or injure, or even to think of it; the sweet and lively emotion which I feel at the sight of all that is virtuous, generous, and amiable; is it possible, I ask, that all these can ever agree in the same heart with the depravity which, without the least scruple, tramples underfoot the sweetest of obligations? No! I feel and loudly assert—it is impossible. Never, for a single moment in his life, could Jean Jacques have been a man without feeling, without compassion, or an unnatural father' (*Confessions*, ii, p. 8).

[2] Cf. *Confessions*, ii, p. 20.

[3] That is to say, he never asked himself, as a result of his concrete experi-

impertinences and the essential disciplines of social living go by the board, without discrimination. Thus what, in certain contexts, can arouse sympathy as springing from a true insight into personal disability (as when he refused to take part in the public affairs of Corsica: 'Fitted by nature to meditate at leisure by myself, I was utterly unfitted to speak, act, and conduct affairs amongst men' (*Confessions*, ii, p. 288), so that, for instance, the tragedy of John Stuart Mill in the House of Commons was not repeated), or can be accepted as providing a genuine revelation of some of the corruptions of eighteenth-century French society, in other situations merely exasperates as a blind egotistical assertion against the wisdom of human knowledge accumulated in certain types of philosophical and dogmatic learning —and this is partly how one tends to react to *Emile*.

Rousseau possessed what, for want of a better term, I must call an 'outsider' mentality. What he has positively to offer depends to a considerable degree on a contradiction of the existing order of things in the society of his time. In *Emile* we are constantly made aware of this; what Rousseau deliberately sets out to provide is an education for some quintessential view of man's nature abstracted from the whole historical context, the characteristic strains, influences and stresses which the historically evolved society of his time might normally be expected to provide. This is partly—but only partly—explicable because of Rousseau's appreciation of the 'restless and uneasy spirit of our times', and of the consequent desire to provide a training which would be useful in all possible mutations of fortune. Rousseau like many modern educationists, is aware of living in an evolving society, one which stresses 'becoming' rather than 'being': '. . . when we consider the fleeting nature of human affairs, the restless and uneasy spirit of our times, when every generation overturns the work of its predecessor, can we conceive a more senseless plan than to educate a child as if he would never leave his room, as if he would always have his servants about

ences, what was involved in the relationship of the individual to the particular historical society in which he was born. He does, of course, give an abstract analysis in the *Contrat Social*.

him?' (*Emile*, p. 10.)[1] The movement towards abstract perfectionism may perhaps represent a grasping after certitude to counterbalance this felt instability of society. Thus Rousseau goes a step further than Locke: Locke thought to impress on the growing mind the modes of the society into which the child was born. He was preparing him for an historically definable status in a period of comparative stability. Rousseau claims—the messianic touch should be noted[2]—to be producing, by his particular set of recommendations, the only true mode of life by aiding man to actualize the 'genuine' potentialities of his nature.

Implicit is a claim to absolute understanding, which is what, in effect, the assertion of the 'natural goodness' of mankind involves; because such a claim assumes that that 'goodness' is knowable in absolute terms and can, by rightful endeavour—or, more accurately, by specific avoidance—be produced.

Thus Rousseau's aim was political in a sense different from Locke's. Locke was prepared largely to accept what is, as 'what is' manifested itself to the consciousness of a well-bred and refined seventeenth-century gentleman at one with the finer awareness of his age.[3] Rousseau wished to form what should be; 'what should be' was conceived, in *Emile*, in absolute and individualistic rather than in contingent and social terms. His ideal was closely bound up with his conviction that political system was the basic reality in forming character: 'I had come to see that everything was radically connected with politics, and that, however one proceeded, no people would be other than the government made it' (*Confessions*, ii, p. 55). A desire to shift

[1] The translation of *Emile* used is that of the Everyman edition.

[2] This note is rarely far absent from 'progressive' philosophies. In Rousseau it appears in individualistic terms. In John Dewey it takes on a social aspect, cf. *My Pedagogic Creed* (Article V): 'But through education society can formulate its own purposes, can organize its own means and resources, and thus shape itself with definiteness and economy in the direction in which it wishes to move.'

[3] It is because the 'finer awareness' of social life in the seventeenth century represented something superior to such social criteria in our own day that we can accept Locke's desiderata in a manner which would be impossible today for current social criteria of education.

responsibility is characteristic of Rousseau. Seventeenth-century society to Locke involved a mode of positive interaction; to Rousseau its incidence is largely negative. The actual, historically evolved society of his time provides a scapegoat to blame for man's inadequacies, a whipping-boy to serve as a protection against the desolations of self-awareness.[1] (That in the *Contrat Social* Rousseau often seems to find his 'freedom' through submission to the social 'general will' need not surprise us. There seems often to be a psychological mechanism which leads the social 'anarchist' (Rousseau, of course, is not quite that) to seek conformity at an abstract level.[2])

Rousseau's general indignation against the 'civilized', as historically manifested in the eighteenth century, does not always display itself as naïvely as in the injunction: 'Reverse the usual practice, and you will almost always do right' (*Emile*, p. 58). It appears in the pervasive sense of being over against current practice, in the subtle self-satisfactions of opposition: 'How people will cry out against me'; or, again: 'I proceed along the

[1] It is interesting to compare the attitude of a stern contemporary critic of Rousseau, Dr. Johnson. In Johnson one sees the profound realization of his own faults and follies and his consequent acceptance of self-responsibility. Thus he inveighs against radical schemes for reform: 'The cure for the greatest part of human miseries is not radical but palliative. Infelicity is involved in corporeal nature, and interwoven with our being; all attempts therefore to decline it wholly are useless and vain: the armies of pain send their arrows against us on every side, the choice is only between those which are more or less sharp, or tinged with poison of greater or less malignity; and the strongest armour which reason can supply, will only blunt their points, but cannot repel them' (*Rambler*, 32). The difference revealed in these expressions of opinion is interestingly displayed in the intimacies of their personal lives. Rousseau's erotic self-indulgences contrast unfavourably with Dr. Johnson's heroic efforts to curb the onslaughts of his own 'vile melancholy' with what seem to have been the sexual peculiarities of their incidence. (Cf. an admirable summary of our knowledge of Johnson's 'deep-rooted psychic maladjustments' in 'Johnson's Vile Melancholy', by K. C. Balderston, printed in *The Age of Johnson*, Essays presented to C. B. Tinker.)

[2] An interesting modern case is that of L. H. Myers. What is interesting in both cases is the rejection of the concrete society manifested in day-to-day living, and the acceptance of the abstract 'disciplined' conformity. (That Myers called his 'conformity' Russia means nothing—Russia, for him, was entirely an abstract conception.)

path which the force of circumstances compels me to tread, but I do not insist that my readers shall follow me. Long ago they have made up their minds that I am wandering in the land of chimeras, while for my part I think they are dwelling in the country of prejudice' (*Emile*, p. 216). It appears in his own assumption of the 'mask' of simplicity: 'Remember, reader, that he who speaks to you is neither a scholar nor a philosopher, but a plain man and a lover of truth; a man who is pledged to no one party or system, a hermit. . . .' (*Emile*, p. 74). It appears in explicit comment on the learned: 'Who can deny that a vast number of things are known to the learned, which the unlearned will never know? Are the learned any nearer truth? Not so, the further they go the further they get from truth, for their pride in their judgment increases faster than their progress in knowledge, so that for every truth they acquire they draw a hundred mistaken conclusions. Every one knows that the learned societies of Europe are mere schools of falsehood, and there are assuredly more mistaken notions in the Academy of Sciences than in a whole tribe of American Indians'[1] (*Emile*, p. 167). It appears, above all, in the appeal, as to a supreme arbiter, to that aspect of the mind with which the individual has, since the time of Rousseau, been increasingly identified, to the exclusion of other features: the feelings, or what has come to be known as the 'heart': 'To exist is to feel; our feeling is undoubtedly earlier than our intelligence, and we had feelings before we had ideas' (*Emile*, p. 253). The subjectivism to which this emphasis on 'feeling' led is revealed in Rousseau's own distinction between 'ideas' and 'feeling': 'When we are chiefly concerned with the object and only think of ourselves as it were by reflection, that is an idea; when, on the other hand, the impression received excites our chief attention and we only think in the second place of the object which caused it, it is a feeling' (*Emile*, footnote, p. 253). Such subjectivism, defined in terms

[1] In considering these statements, Rousseau's incapacity for prolonged study needs to be borne in mind. (Cf. *Confessions*, i, pp. 215–18.) In his defence, it must be said that he was expressing more forcefully a common theme of the eighteenth century—the distrust of learning as pedantic and superfluous. 'Common-sense' was thought to be a sufficient guide.

of the particularly relaxed nature of Rousseau's 'feeling', its equation with 'rêverie' of the debilitating nature examined above,[1] has had an important influence in the decay of the European tradition. Too often it has been forgotten that the emotional, as well as the intellectual, life has its precisions and exactness. Great poetry contains the story of these; and it is characteristic of such poetry that it should achieve a measure of 'impersonality', not simply represent the subjectivity of the writer. Rousseau's appreciation of the importance of the emotional life is marred by the terms in which he conceives it.

It would naturally follow, from what has been said about Rousseau's concern for an unhistorical conception of man, that one of the interesting features of the child Emile would emerge in his being a child in the abstract: 'We must therefore look at the general rather than the particular, and consider our scholar as man in the abstract, man exposed to all the changes and chances of mortal life' (*Emile*, p. 10). In addition he is to be an 'ordinary' child: 'It is ordinary people who have to be educated, and their education alone can serve as a pattern for the education of their fellows. The others find their way alone' (*Emile*, p. 19)—where one marks an early exposition of that idea so frequently encountered today that 'ordinary' or 'backward' children are more difficult to teach than clever children.[2]

Emile is an abstraction of a particularly interesting kind. In the first place, Jean-Jacques is quite blind to the lessons of memory, to the understanding of his own childhood;[3] he draws no strength from that 'seed-time' of his own soul such as makes Wordsworth's insight into childhood so remarkably perceptive.

[1] Cf. too: 'I am led by long-standing habit to those upliftings of the heart, which do not impose upon me the trouble of thinking.'

[2] Of course, they are not. They merely require a different sort of attention. Clever children, *properly instructed,* make intense demands on the insight and intellectual capacity of the teacher.

[3] I shall be mostly concerned, in this essay, with Rousseau's recommendations for the pre-adolescent child. When Emile reached the age of fifteen or sixteen, when puberty, 'that stormy period of change which is forecast by indications of growing passions', Rousseau, as is well known, advocated a different approach—equally inadequate, I would add—to which brief reference will be made later.

Thus, when speaking in the *Confessions* of the discrepancy between his own appreciation as a child, of God, and his repudiation of any teaching of the idea of God to children, he asserts: 'If I have said that we ought not to speak about religion to children, if we wish them to possess any, and, further, that they are incapable of knowing God, even according to our ideas, I have drawn this conviction from my observations, not from my own experience, for I knew that no conclusions could be drawn from it in regard to others. Find me Jean Jacques Rousseaus of six years old, and speak to *them* of God when they are seven; I will guarantee that you run no risk' (*Confessions*, i, p. 54). The human 'nature', then, which Rousseau wished to cultivate in his Emile is the fruit of external observation of a quasi-scientific and therefore restricted, purview; it does not spring from an intuitive understanding based on self-experience and self-understanding.

Rousseau's awareness of child nature as different from that of the adult has deservedly been noted as constituting an important advance in educational possibilities. That, 'Nature would have them children before they are men. . . . Childhood has its own ways of seeing, thinking, and feeling; nothing is more foolish than to try and substitute our ways' (*Emile*, p. 54), has become one of the staple clichés of current educational precept. It formed no such feature of eighteenth-century thought, and Rousseau deserves praise for having emphasized it. The more normal practice was to regard the child as a young adult, ready to be shaped and moulded according to the prevailing social mode of gentlemanliness. At the same time, Rousseau's recognition of childhood as an autonomous state carried with it implications which have been too little considered. At least the recognition of the child as a young adult implied that, potentially at least, the child was as complex as the man. Paradoxically, Rousseau's splitting of child and adult nature has carried with it at once a complication and a simplification; a complication because the child and the man have come to take on two separate and distinct identities; the teacher has become much more self-conscious about his task. The child has demanded recognition as a separate entity with 'rights' of his own; thus that tendency to separate, to categorize, to divide off has received an added impetus, with some gain and some loss to both adult and child. But there has also been a simplification, because the child that Rousseau wished to educate was so much simpler in nature than the adult that Rousseau himself, for instance, was; and something of this tendency towards simplification has persisted in post-Rousseau theorizing. The child has, in fact, been sentimentalized, a feature which can be seen in Rousseau's embarrassingly rhapsodical accounts of what Emile becomes as a result of his upbringing: 'But when I think of a child of ten or twelve, strong, healthy, well-grown for his age, only pleasant thoughts are called up, whether of the present or the future. I see him keen, eager, and full of life, free from gnawing cares and painful forebodings, absorbed in this present state, and delighting in a fullness of life which seems to extend beyond himself. I look forward to a time when he will use his daily increasing sense, intelligence and vigour, those growing powers of which he continually gives fresh proof. I watch the child with delight, I picture to myself the man with even greater pleasure. His eager life seems to stir my own pulses, I seem to live his life and in his vigour I renew my own' (*Emile*, p. 123). The last sentence perhaps, provides a clue, for it reveals the educator's all too frequently expressed desire to find satisfaction *through* the children; so much of the simplification of child nature that one so often notes springs from the naïve belief that the life more abundant can come with the next generation, that some mode of instruction can supply the easier road to maturity and thus compensate, even if only vicariously, the adult for present discontents. Rousseau begins a sentimentalizing of the situation which has bedevilled child study down to our own day.[1]

[1] Not all writers about children, of course, show quite the innocence of James Hemming and Josephine Balls, when they state: 'If parents find their child in a "bad" gang, they should look for the cause in home or school life, not in Tom's or Margery's nature' (*The Child is Right*, p. 147). Thus, Lewis Carroll is remarkably unsentimental about Alice; and D. H. Lawrence saw the 'oh-so-spiteful look' as well as the 'oh-so-spiritual look'. Though the conviction of original sin induced a belief in child depravity of

Thus, what is interesting about Emile is the combination of observation and 'idealization'—idealization both in the sense of pursuing that which is looked upon as most desirable, and in D. H. Lawrence's sense of working in terms of an abstract conception of the thing. The inhibiting effects of Jean Jacques's self-regard and lack of self-knowledge display themselves; he cannot fully appreciate child nature because he cannot really see it as bearing much resemblance to his own—'no conclusions could be drawn from it in regard to others': he must trust to external observation and thus simplify: 'The child must come first, and you must devote yourself entirely to him. Watch him, study him constantly, without his knowing it.' It cannot ultimately be as satisfactory as observation implemented by self-awareness because there is no standard of reference for interpretation. It is a curious paradox that many who have depended so much on the inner life (Froebel is another example who springs to mind) have shown so little awareness of it in others, and of its possible corruptions.

Rousseau called his 'idealization' the 'natural man'; to arrive at some more precise understanding of what he implied by 'natural' and by 'nature' will help to indicate more concretely the sort of individual he attempted to form and that individual's relations with his environment.

The word 'nature' is one of protean ambiguity, and Rousseau himself uses it in a number of different senses. The term has exercised a great influence in many fields of thought, including that of educational theory.[1] One sense in which Rousseau uses

absurd proportions, the current tendency to blame so many faults on the environment—or the parents—or something or somebody outside the child contains equal possibilities of excess. At the same time, the child's responsibility always remains less than the adult's; to that extent, at least, his egotism is more innocent. And it is part of the educator's job to wean him from that concern with self, to give him that faculty of 'attention' (cf. Simone Weil, *Waiting on God*) without which mental and spiritual growth is impossible.

[1] Some of the most interesting elucidations are to be found among Arthur Lovejoy's articles in *Essays in the History of Ideas*. Cf. also, Professor Basil Willey's *Eighteenth Century Background*. An admirable chapter in Professor C. D. Hardie's *Truth and Fallacy in Educational Theory*, 'Education according to Nature', analyses a number of propositions which are implicit in Rous-

'nature' is to designate the phenomenal world apart from man, especially the world of plants and animals. Thus, in speaking of the custom of adding wine to the warm water in which the infant is first bathed, he asserts that 'I think the wine might be dispensed with. As nature does not produce fermented liquors, it is not likely that they are of much value to her creatures' (*Emile*, pp. 26–7). Such a meaning is implied by his analogies drawn from animal life: the example, for instance, of the way in which puppies practise their budding teeth. Such a conception of 'nature' not only has the power, often, of positive example; it also provides the permanent background of instruction and observation:

'Men are not made to be crowded together in ant-hills, but scattered over the earth to till it. . . .

'Men are devoured by our towns. In a few generations the race dies out or becomes degenerate; it needs renewal, and it is always renewed from the country' (*Emile*, p. 26).

It also forms the subject-matter of learning, through observation of the behaviour of 'natural' objects: 'Teach your scholar to observe the phenomena of nature; you will soon rouse his curiosity. . . . Let him not be taught science, let him discover it' (*Emile*, p. 131). It is important to realize, once more, that Rousseau drew no deep resources of wisdom, as did Wordsworth, from an appreciation of man's organic relationship with this 'nature'. There is no sense of fusion, no wisdom derived from the 'imaginative' apprehension of the 'Wisdom and Spirit' of the Universe; no 'plastic power', permitting

> *observations of affinities*
> *In objects where no brother-hood exists*
> *To passive minds,*

moved Rousseau's soul in subservience 'strictly to external things'. 'Nature', in this sense, for Rousseau, seems to have provided either a background for fantasy life, a retreat and a 'solitude' in which he did not have to face up to the responsibili-

seau's work, and should be consulted. Cf. also, J. Maritain, *Trois Reformateurs*, which contains an essay on Rousseau.

ties of social living: 'I sometimes exclaimed with emotion, "O Nature! O my mother! behold me under thy protection alone! Here there is no cunning or knavish mortal to thrust himself between me and thee" ' (*Confessions*, ii, p. 282), or to have provided the material for a series of observations of a biological or botanical kind which could be applied more or less mechanically (at least with too little concern for the implications of some of the analogies) to the education of the 'natural' man; or to have afforded a subject-matter for control and investigation in the manner indicated by such sources of prudential management as *Robinson Crusoe*, a book Rousseau is concerned to recommend as supplying 'the best treatise on natural education'; and, as we shall see, a great deal of Rousseau's education is intended to make the child at home in the midst of this 'natural' environment.[1]

[1] In an extremely interesting article on *Robinson Crusoe as a Myth* (*Essays in Criticism*, Vol. i, No. 2, April 1951), Mr. Ian Watt seems to pay too little attention to this ambiguity of attitude in Rousseau's approach to 'wild nature'. Thus, he contrasts Defoe's use of nature, in *Robinson Crusoe*, as matter for exploitation, self-help, purposive possession and colonial development with Rousseau's interpretation of the book in *Emile* as an example of solitary pastoral retreat for self-communion. In actual fact, it is the self-help aspect of *Robinson Crusoe*, which appeals to Rousseau for, as I have pointed out, his attitude to 'nature' in this sense involves at times a background for self-indulgence and at times material for 'exploitation'; and it is the latter which his use of Defoe's book is intended to advocate. There is a great deal of Defoe's ethos, which Mr. Watt interestingly defines, in Rousseau's educational ideas; his 'negative' education is largely a means not to idleness but precisely to self-help and discovery on the part of the pupil; and the virtue which he finds in the savage is not that of blissful peace but the necessity 'to reason at every step he takes. He can neither move nor walk without considering the consequences' (*Emile*, p. 83). Cf. Rousseau's comments on *Robinson Crusoe* (*Emile*, pp. 147–8)—particularly: 'This novel, stripped of irrelevant matter, begins with Robinson's shipwreck on his island and ends with the coming of the ship which bears him from it, and it will furnish Emile with material, both for work and play, during the whole period we are considering. His head should be full of it, he should always be busy with his castle, his goats, his plantations. Let him learn in detail, not from books but from things, all that is necessary in such a case. Let him think he is Robinson himself; . . . he should anxiously consider what steps to take; will this or that be wanting. He should examine his hero's conduct. . . .' Indeed, the passage that Mr. Watt quotes from *Robinson Crusoe* sets out admirably

Several other equally significant meanings of 'nature' and 'natural', need to be indicated. Thus, 'natural' comes to signify 'that which is in accord with the behaviour of primitive, pre-civilized, savage man' (though this meaning is not as frequent as some commentators on Rousseau have made out). Hence, in expatiating on the desire for self-preservation, he remarks: 'In a natural state man is only eager to preserve his life while he has the means for its preservation; when self-preservation is no longer possible, he resigns himself to his fate and dies without vain torments. Nature teaches the first law of resignation. Savages, like wild beasts, make very little struggle against death, and meet it almost without a murmur. When this natural law is overthrown reason establishes another, but few discern it, and man's resignation is never so complete as nature's (*Emile*, p. 46). (The division between the law of nature and that of reason is worth noting.) Hence nature sometimes comes to mean 'that which is opposed to nurture, to all training given by other men': 'Drawn this way by nature and that way by man, compelled to yield to both forces, we make a compromise and reach neither goal' (*Emile*, p. 9). Also, it takes on the significance of 'that which is opposed to historical situation'. Thus, in speaking of matters of religion, immediately after the testimony of the Savoyard Vicar, Rousseau states: 'So long as we yield nothing to human authority, nor to the prejudices of our native land, the light of reason alone, in a state of nature, can lead us no further than to natural religion' (*Emile*, p. 278). And Rousseau's 'natural religion' involves a further important meaning: 'that which can be deduced from the abstract psychological tendencies common to all men'. There is the Vicar's

that conception of rational invention which Rousseau permits to the child: 'By making and acquiring everything by reason and by making the most rational judgments of things, every man may be in time master of every mechanic art. I had never handled a tool in my life, and yet in time by labour, application and contrivance I found at least that I wanted nothing but I could have made it; especially if I had had the tools.' Mr. Watt interestingly reveals the fallacy of the desert island existence, how, in fact, those who really suffered such exposure to 'nature' reverted to an almost animal state of existence or went mad.

testimony: 'all that man knows by nature I am capable of knowing' (*Emile*, p. 261).

There is now emerging a conscious view of human nature, one in which 'conscience' and 'reason' play a predominant part and which therefore leads 'naturally' to a certain type of deistic belief. Here, Rousseau draws on the uniformitarian beliefs of the eighteenth century; the 'natural man' comes to be equivalent to the 'real' man discoverable under all forms and pretences; he is equated with those common gifts, those rules discovered 'at the very centre of my being, indelibly inscribed by nature', behind all the 'masks' which ordinary social life provides to hide a man's 'true' nature: 'Hitherto I have made no distinction of condition, rank, station, or fortune; nor shall I distinguish between them in the future, since man is the same in every station; the rich man's stomach is no bigger than the poor man's, nor is his digestion any better; . . . a great man is no taller than one of the people, and indeed the natural needs are the same to all, and the means of satisfying them should be equally within the reach of all. Fit a man's education to his real self, not to what is no part of him' (*Emile*, pp. 156–7).

Thus, we arrive at the significance: 'that which is in line with a certain order of human development through which Rousseau believes that man realizes his true inner potentialities'. This is probably the heart of the conception of 'natural man'. No human regression to a primitive state is intended, but the achievement of a harmony between man and his environment through which man will attain his true happiness and 'being'. *L'amour de soi-même* was to be encouraged and *amour-propre* avoided, which latter, as Rousseau pointed out in the *Discourse on Inequality*, was a 'factitious feeling, arising only in society, which leads each man to think more highly of himself than of any other.' This last significance of 'nature' is implicit in such comments as: 'l'homme naturel est pour lui,' and: 'Before his parents chose a calling for him nature called him to be a man. Life is the trade I would teach him. When he leaves me, I grant you, he will be neither a magistrate, a soldier, nor a priest; he will be a man. All that becomes a man he will learn as quickly as another. In vain will fate change his station, he will always be in his right place' (*Emile*, p. 9). And, of course, in practice, this meaning often equates itself with that 'order of human existence which Rousseau, for a variety of reasons, considers desirable'. This meaning harmonizes all the rest; if we bear in mind the characteristic stresses of Rousseau's work rather than individual phrases torn from context (the products frequently of an ill-adjusted vehemence), it enables us to summarize his ultimate conception of human life, to which Emile's education is directed. Thus, whereas it is true that the savage state is not in Rousseau's eyes the most desirable, and he believes that man must learn to live among other men, the general emphasis of his work in *Emile* is to depreciate the social, the sophisticated, the urban, the 'civilized' in the sense which is prepared to accept conventional forms of society and conventional disciplines of learning through books and the traditions built up by others, and to stress man's need to learn from a carefully selected series of observations drawn from animal and especially rustic life, and thus to follow some quintessential conception of manhood beneath all the forms of conventional existence and the particular trainings implied in such social occupations, to accept the discipline of 'things', to maintain an independence of others and to find in practical utility the true criterion of learning, to prefer the less sophisticated forms of human activity to the more: 'Now, of all the pursuits by which a man may earn his living, the nearest to a state of nature is manual labour' (*Emile*, p. 158).[1]

As Arthur Lovejoy has said, for Rousseau 'man's good lay in departing from his "natural" (in the sense of primitive, savage) state—but not too much; "perfectibility" up to a certain point was desirable, though beyond that point an evil. Not its infancy but its *jeunesse* was the best age of the human race.'[2] Rousseau

[1] Cf. *Emile*, p. 151: '. . . the art which is most generally useful and necessary, is undoubtedly that which most deserves esteem, and that art which requires the least help from others, is more worthy of honour than those which are dependent on other arts, since it is freer and more nearly independent. These are the true laws of value in the arts; all others are arbitrary and dependent on popular prejudice.'

[2] Arthur Lovejoy, 'The Supposed Primitivism of Rousseau's Discourse on

wants, in fact, the imagined freedom of a simpler life ('Emile, having been brought up in full freedom like young peasants and savages'[1]) with such advantages of civilization as are necessary to preserve a certain competence. He sees none of the disadvantages of the simple life, the essential strains of living, in whatever context. Nor does he appreciate the profound difficulties of tacking on this type of existence to the historically evolved society of his time, a society which, by its very existence, makes certain demands, involves certain inherited modes and memories of living which cannot simply be ignored or forgotten. Such modes form the essential background against which any idea of 'reform' must measure itself or at least accept as primary data. This aspect of Rousseau's 'romanticism' has affected modern educational thinking which, in certain of its manifestations, looks to the lifting of restraint as the essential element in the truly educative process.

Emile, of course, is directed towards indicating how this ideal, 'natural' and, in effect, highly abstract, human being could be produced. This explains the cryptic letter to Cramer:

'You say, quite rightly, that it is impossible to produce an Emile; but do you really believe that that was my aim and that the book which carries such a title is a treatise on education? It's a work basically philosophical on the principle put forward by the author in other writings that man is naturally good.

'To bring this notion into line with another, no less certain, truth, that men are evil, it was necessary to show how all the vices developed in the human heart. This is what I have done in this book. . . .'[2] (13th October 1764.)

For, in indicating how the 'natural' man should be formed, Rousseau was largely concerned with what should be avoided so that man's evil propensities should not be permitted to develop.

Inequality', reprinted in *Essays in the History of Ideas*. By 'perfectibility' Lovejoy refers to social conceptions of perfection. Rousseau, of course, as is implied, has his own perfectionism.

[1] *Emile*, p. 288.

[2] Cf. *Emile*, p. 56: 'Let us lay it down as an incontrovertible rule that the

The basic inadequacy of *Emile* lies in its treatment of human egotism. One can see, in fact, that the need to assert the natural goodness of man, and the consequent distortions of emphasis which such an assertion has entailed, have thrown the whole treatment of education out of gear. For it has forced Rousseau to adopt what is, in effect, a highly artificial system, and to assert a rigid dichotomy between man and society which has no basis in experience and which immediately perverts the 'practical' possibilities of the treatise. It begins with the highly disputable dogmatic assertion that childish egotism comes from ill-teaching, not from 'nature': 'This is how they become tiresome, masterful, imperious, naughty, and unmanageable; a development which does not spring from a natural love of power, but one which has been taught them, for it does not need much experience to realize how pleasant it is to set others to work and to move the world by a word' (*Emile*, p. 34). How that which is not there can be evoked even by bad training is a possible sophistication that Rousseau does not appreciate.[1] Even Rousseau, however, has to admit that egotism (*amour-propre*, or *fantaisie*) is unavoidable in society; he is thus forced to impose a peculiar isolation on both tutor and child, and to demand a perceptiveness on the part of the tutor, whose function it is to '. . . study carefully their speech and gestures, so that at an age when they are incapable of deceit you may discriminate between those desires which come from nature and those which spring from perversity' (*Emile*, p. 35), which could only be adequately fulfilled by someone having superhuman powers of intuition. And, indeed, Rousseau, by stressing the necessity of meeting the true 'needs' of children: 'He is only subject to others because of his needs, and because they see better than he what he really needs, what may help or hinder his existence' (*Emile*, p. 48), avoids, as does so much current educational theorizing, the precise assessment of what constitutes a human

first impulses of nature are always right; there is no original sin in the human heart, the how and why of the entrance of every vice can be traced.'

[1] 'Progressive' educationists, following Rousseau's abstraction of responsibility from the child, often make extremely naîve assessments of child nature.

'need'. Thus it was an important step on Rousseau's part to stress the need for child activity, as, for instance, against the pervasive tyranny of the *maillot*; what is insufficiently valid is the ultimate end which this activity is intended to subserve; moreover he neglects the equally valid need for receptivity. Thus, what I am concerned to criticize is not the importance of Rousseau's stress on the necessity to consider the 'needs' of children, but the fact that in Rousseau these 'needs' are stressed in relationship to a too inadequate conception of the nature of life and of the ends of human existence—an inadequacy briefly indicated above. One needs to temper praise for Rousseau's perceptiveness in recognizing children's 'needs' with a regret that such 'needs' were not stressed by one whose realization of need at any stage of existence was supplemented by a fuller appreciation of such need in relation to end; the second term in Rousseau's diagnosis: 'because they see better than he what he really needs' is the weaker link in his argument.[1]

It is important to appreciate the effect of Rousseau's emphasis on the education of 'things'; even the tutor is to become a 'thing' in order to avoid arousing the egotism of the child: 'Keep the child dependent on things only. By this course of education you will have followed the order of nature' (*Emile*, p. 49). One obvious advantage Rousseau derives from making the tutor like a 'thing' lies in avoiding the possibility of those emotional disturbances between pupil and tutor which his own experience as a teacher had revealed to him: '. . . when things went wrong, I was a devil. When my pupils did not understand me, I raved like a madman; when they showed signs of insubordination, I could have killed them, which was not the way to

[1] It is the precise assessment in concrete situations of what a child 'needs'—a problem which, once the child has grown beyond the predominantly biological stage, in most contexts, raises fundamental philosophical issues concerning the ends of human existence, and which educationalists show too little willingness to tackle—which constitutes the value of thinking, educationally, in terms of such 'needs'. Psychological assessments of these 'needs' all too frequently draw attention to the mental presuppositions—and limitations—of the psychologists. And a pervasive stress on physical activity has followed too frequently the Rousseauesque assumption: 'let him be a man in strength and he will soon be one in reason' (p. 111).

make them either learned or well-disposed. (*Confessions*, i, pp. 245–6.)[1]

In his concrete recommendations, Rousseau falls into that verbal ambiguity which dogs the progress of modern education. He intends to free the child, on the grounds we have noted that 'the first impulses of nature are always right; there is no original sin in the human heart' (*Emile*, p. 56). Thus, he urges such precepts as: 'The only habit the child should be allowed to contract is that of having no habits' (p. 30), which obviously form an important element in the idea of 'negative education': 'Give nature time to work before you take over her business, lest you interfere with her dealings' (*Emile*, p. 71). Yet, at the same time, there is implicit in many of his recommendations an active human authoritative interference. The sort of environment in which the child is to be placed is to be chosen most carefully: 'As soon as the child begins to take notice, what is shown to him must be carefully chosen' (*Emile*, p. 30). Even more explicit is the recommendation: 'While the child is still unconscious there is time to prepare his surroundings, so that nothing shall strike his eye but what is fit for his sight' (*Emile*, p. 59). A great deal of this is consistent with modern practice, and provides one of the sources from which modern education has learnt its technique of infant management. From such precepts springs that confusion of freedom and authority characteristic of many modern expositions. Rousseau himself is led to his ambiguous position because of his assumption that man only learns evil from others.

To learn from 'things' has none of those disadvantages to which learning from men lay itself open; for 'it is in man's

[1] Rousseau deserves credit, at least, for his perception that such reactions on his part were not the best way of making his pupils 'learned and well-disposed'. At the same time, his belief that contact with things will never arouse the child's egotism and that the child will accept the discipline of things without resentment shows a surprising lack of observation. Cf. 'It looks as if there was a universal tendency to include physical things in the society of living things and to respond to them as such' (W. J. H. Sprott, *Social Psychology*). Certainly, young children make no clear distinction between animate and inanimate objects.

nature to bear patiently with the nature of things, but not with the ill-will of another' (*Emile*, p. 55). At the same time, he realizes that some order of presentation is necessary to the growing mind and explicitly admits that the child is so feeble that 'il craint tout ce qu'il ne connaît pas' (*Emile*, p. 37). He must thus smuggle in a human intervention which is confined to the careful presentation of data, but which is, none the less, real for all the apparent restriction of its incidence. The most perfect example of this ambivalence of Rousseau's attitude occurs when he asserts that Emile 'should always do what he wants to do, but he should only want to do what you want him to do'. One is reminded that Rousseau was the originator of Totalitarian as well as of Liberal Democracy.[1] And, indeed, *Emile* is much more subtly authoritarian than might at first appear.

Thus the idea of learning from the environment, of subservience to the authority of 'things' rather than of people was considerably advanced by this eighteenth-century writer's indignation against a society with which he was unable to come to terms. He was aided by the pervasive tendency of the time to find in sense experience, the source of scientific understanding, the chief source of 'real' knowledge. (Both Comenius—following Bacon—and Locke had urged the vital importance of learning through the senses; such learning formed the basis of Locke's psychology.) Knowledge, according to Rousseau, was either sensational or intuitive; it came either from the environment, or from the intuitive perceptions of the 'Inner Light'; other people, the authority imposed by conventional, social and intellectual arrangements constituted the danger to the integral and pure heart of man. Modern education, largely unaware of the origin of its techniques, emerges from a shift in assumptions about man's nature which stresses at once his conceit of himself in terms of innate goodness, and his uniform capability to learn; and one strain in modern egalitarianism springs as much from the conception that everything which comes from others spells corruption (is, in fact, a protective device) as it does from a positive belief in man's equality of endowment. It finds its

[1] Cf. J. L. Talmon, *Totalitarian Democracy*.

roots in a desire to shift responsibility for evil on to others; and that desire to shift responsibility on to something other than self is peculiarly characteristic of Rousseau's own psychology. In this, he is a true representative figure of the modern world.[1]

Rousseau's exposition of the learning process disingenuously fails to discriminate between two sorts of learning. There is the learning involved in biological development, the need for activity so that muscles, etc., can expand: 'Let them run, jump and shout to their heart's content' (*Emile*, p. 50). Such learning is, of course, largely spontaneous; it needs to be distinguished from that mental learning which results from perception and realization of the environment, where spontaneity and nurture intermingle in a way which requires more careful elucidation than Rousseau seems to realize:

'Without the study of books, such a memory as the child may possess is not left idle; everything he sees and hears makes an impression on him, he keeps a record of men's sayings and doings, and his whole environment is the book from which he unconsciously enriches his memory, till his judgment is able to profit by it.

'To select these objects, to take care to present him constantly with those he may know, to conceal from him those he ought not to know, this is the real way of training his early memory' (*Emile*, p. 76).

Organic development, maturation, will go on to a certain extent irrespective of usage (though, even here, development will be better if there *is* usage, and Rousseau seems to be aware of this, for he emphasizes the need for physical exercise and movement).[2] Mental growth only proceeds from usage and conscious

[1] Cf. Reinhold Niebuhr, *The Nature of Man*, particularly Chapter IV, entitled 'The Easy Conscience of Modern Man'. Very relevant is Rousseau's extraordinary account of how he settled the matter of his own salvation by throwing a stone at a tree, cf. *Confessions*, i, p. 223.

[2] The position is perhaps best summed up in a brief introduction to the study of mental measurement, published in *An Introduction to Modern Psychology* by O. L. Zangwill. Professor Zangwill is there drawing on the researches of Gesell and others: 'In "learning to walk" maturation is far more important than practice; in "learning to talk", on the other hand, practice is

employment, once the necessary organic development has taken place; there is something ambiguous in the injunction: 'The mind should be left undisturbed till its faculties have developed' (*Emile*, p. 57). And from the ensuing remarks, it is obvious that Rousseau is confusing the two sorts of growth: 'If only you could let well alone, and get others to follow your example; if you could bring your scholar to the age of twelve strong and healthy, but unable to tell his right hand from his left, the eyes of his understanding would be open to reason as soon as you began to teach him. Free from prejudices and free from habits, there would be nothing in him to counteract the effects of your labours. In your hands he would soon become the wisest of men; by doing nothing to begin with, you would end with a prodigy of education' (*Emile*, pp. 57–8). Without exercise of mental 'faculties' there is no intellectual growth at all: Rousseau's following of nature involves too rigid an application of analogy from organic development. It is not true that mental growth follows the same patterns, and that the policy of non-interference in the one will have equally good results in the other; only skilled intervention can bring to mental maturity, can, even within the limited purview of Rousseau's conception of experience, bring about the appreciation of stress and importance.

Moreover, it is important to note the implications of the sort of 'reason' involved in this type of learning. Emile's earlier education is very much one of learning 'how things work', of gaining a measure of control over his environment; and the sort of 'reason' which Rousseau allows to pre-adolescent children is that which enables them to see relations of sense experience. The need for *present* interest is stressed. The possible contingencies of a later period are to be ignored, for the child may die at any time, and preparation for such a hypothetical future would be so much time wasted. The type of education desiderated is one which will help the child to be at home in the world

everything—provided that the requisite stage of developmental readiness has been reached' (p. 147). We cannot be reminded of this simple truth too often.

in the here and now. 'On the other hand, he exercises discrimination and forethought, he reasons about everything that concerns himself. He does not chatter, he acts. Not a word does he know of what is going on in the world at large, but he knows very thoroughly what affects himself. As he is always stirring he is compelled to notice many things, to recognize many effects; he soon acquires a good deal of experience. Nature, not man, is his schoolmaster, and he learns all the quicker because he is not aware that he has any lesson to learn. So mind and body work together. He is always carrying out his own ideas, not those of other people, and thus he unites thought and action; as he grows in health and strength he grows in wisdom and discernment' (*Emile*, p. 84). In this way, the only sort of reason of which Rousseau considers children are capable is developed, for: 'our first teachers in natural philosophy are our feet, hands, and eyes. To substitute books for them does not teach us to reason, it teaches us to use the reason of others rather than our own' (*Emile*, p. 90).

There are several points worth noting about this type of education. It involves a principle of considerable importance, one in which there is a certain degree of psychological truth and one which modern education has not been slow to take advantage of. Nevertheless, learning by this kind of discovery develops only certain approaches to the nature of experience; it helps the 'practically'-minded child. But the world of practical experience does not involve the whole of the human potentiality, even where pre-adolescent children are concerned; and even within its limited purview, Rousseau depends overmuch on the assumed 'spontaneous' curiosity of the child—and the child's ability to appreciate points of significance in what is presented. The *Robinson Crusoe* approach is artificial in normal community life because it assumes a motivation lacking outside the pressure to survival on desert islands. There is too little obligation on the child to 'reason' even in the way which is allowed him, and, indeed, too much reliance seems to be placed on incidental encounters which happen to throw into the way temporary inducements for learning. Present interest and a certain natural curiosity, the twin bastions of Rousseau's system, do not always have the efficacy that is alleged on their behalf. Thus it is not true, necessarily, that 'every concrete example suggests another and always points to the next in the series. This succession, which stimulates the curiosity and so arouses the attention required by every object in turn, is the order followed by most men, and it is the right order for all children' (*Emile*, p. 135). Such a generalization depends too much on culturally induced conceptions of cause and effect. The appreciation of a chain of relationships is no more 'natural' than any other mode of systematizing phenomena or of inducing some method of order into the presented chaos of sense impression. Furthermore, the importance of language is overlooked.

Again, too much emphasis is placed on novelty of discovery. For instance, Rousseau, in his example of the magnet and the duck, an experiment which is supposed to lead to the study of physics, assumes a power of generalizing in the child only possible to those who are already habituated to the mode of drawing general inferences from the observation of a number of individual phenomena, or of otherwise relating phenomena which, unaided, he would not necessarily connect: 'Let the child learn all these facts, let him learn those that are within his reach by experiment, and discover the rest by induction; but I would far rather he knew nothing at all about them, than that you should tell him' (*Emile*, p. 113). Thus, to make the leap from the observation of the behaviour of the duck to the discovery of the compass ('the study of physics has begun') implies a mental leap which can only result from a certain type of conscious training inhibited by Rousseau's injunctions.

Again, the general principle enunciated in the following is certainly untrue: 'Undoubtedly the notions of things thus acquired for oneself are clearer and much more convincing than those acquired from the teaching of others; and not only is our reason not accustomed to a slavish submission to authority, but we develop greater ingenuity in discovering relations, connecting ideas and inventing apparatus, than when we merely accept what is given us and allow our minds to be enfeebled by indifference' (*Emile*, p. 139). Not only are there certain types of learning which can only be attained on the word of others, and which such a principle would remove from the 'syllabus' (an omission which Rousseau, to do him justice, is prepared to face); it is certainly not true that 'it is only objects which can be perceived by the senses which can have any interest for children'.[1] In objecting to verbal explanation, Rousseau was revolting with good reason against an over-verbal type of education; but he reacted too far. He completely banishes imaginative literature for young children, for instance. His comment on the fable of La Fontaine involves a notorious literalness of interpretation which it is safe to assume children are not bothered about; (the empirical argument about the distance at which a cheese can be smelt is sufficient to illustrate the criteria brought to bear by Rousseau). The apposite comment, the product of a mind working on a very different level of imaginative insight, is that of Coleridge: 'For from my early reading of fairy tales and genii, etc., etc., my mind had been habituated *to the Vast*, and I never regarded *my senses* in any way as the criteria of my belief. I regulated all my creeds by my conceptions, not by my sight, even at that age. Should children be permitted to read romances, and relations of giants and magicians and genii? I know all that has been said against it; but I have formed my faith in the affirmative. I know no other way of giving the mind a love of the Great and the Whole. Those who have been led to the same truths step by step, through the constant testimony of their senses, seem to me to want a sense which I possess. They contemplate nothing but *parts*, and all *parts* are necessarily little. And the universe to them is but a mass of *little things*. It is true, that the mind *may* become credulous and prone to superstition by the former method; but are not the experimentalists credulous even to madness in believing any absurdity, rather than believe the grandest truths, if they have not the testimony of their own senses in their favour? I have known some who have been rationally educated, as it is styled. They were marked by a microscopic acuteness, but when they looked at

[1] *Emile*, p. 140.

great things, all became a blank and they saw nothing, and denied (very illogically) that anything could be seen, and uniformly put the negation of a power for the possession of a power, and called the want of imagination judgment and the never being moved to rapture philosophy!' (Letter to Poole, 16th October 1797.) It is significant that Rousseau, himself so influenced as a child by romantic literature, should be opposed to any imaginative reading by the child, not on the grounds that children should be kept from certain types of literature (a prohibition which Jean-Jacques might well support from personal experience) but because he is concerned to omit altogether the need for the sort of training that literature can supply.

Thus Rousseau constantly inveighs against book learning: 'Reading is the scourge of childhood,' and 'Books! What sorry clutter for a child of that age.' He claims that he is allowing the child to gather the skills of learning: 'You teach science; well and good; I am busy fashioning the necessary tools for its acquisition' (*Emile*, p. 90). Yet one of the chief skills, that of reading, is deprecated. It is quite unjustifiable to urge that 'The child who reads does not think. He only knows how to read' (*Emile*, p. 179), as should be obvious enough. Reading can set up an 'activity' in the mind, no less inferior to that provided by environmental stimuli. Like many 'progressive' educationalists Rousseau is too taken up with physical activity to appreciate the full value of mental exercise. Rousseau's emphasis on the 'natural' man leads, in fact, to a misconception of man's nature;[1] what was 'natural' to man, as an older view made clear, was precisely his capacity for complex development, his ability to respond to training and nurture, his building up on an assimilation of previous knowledge and wisdom; this most obviously marks him off from the animals.

The implications of Rousseau's own peculiar psychology, then, are becoming clearer; his theory of 'negative' education involves basically an unwillingness to measure up to the full

[1] Cf. Niebuhr, op. cit.: '. . . the great achievement of modern culture, the understanding of nature, is also the cause of the great confusion of modern man: the misunderstanding of human nature' (p. 101).

complexities involved in growing up in society. The education of 'things' avoids all those complications of egotism and emotion which are specifically characteristic of man and through which a child must develop. Rousseau's pedagogy, in *Emile*, like some modern theorizing, is one of self-development and evolution rather than of conflict involving self-transcendence; and such straightforward evolution can only exist within a system which ignores many of the incongruities inherent in the development of human beings. He is concerned to eliminate conflict from his scheme—the education of things 'being non-moral does no injury to liberty and begets no vices'.[1] The same desire is manifested in the bringing up of adolescents, who, no longer free, even in Rousseau's view, from the possibilities of emotional disturbances, are yet to be sheltered from emotional experience: 'we must take the opposite way from that hitherto followed, and instruct the youth rather through the experience of others than through his own' (*Emile*, p. 198). Yet, as Keats pointed out, only out of such experience can maturity come: 'axioms in philosophy are not axioms until they are proved upon our pulses.' The choice of Sophie through the tutor has often been commented upon as one of the less happy recommendations of Rousseau; yet its significance has been little realized. It represents yet another aspect of Rousseau's fear of emotional complication. It demonstrates how little he learnt from such emotional situations as they affected his own life. His whole picture of the Emile-Sophie relationship is marred by an inhibiting sentimentality which seems to indicate how little Rousseau understood about such relationships; even 'reverie', to deserve attention requires, a somewhat closer contact with life as we know it than Rousseau displays.

The implication, in *Emile*, then, all too frequently is that ignorance implies innocence and virtue; an assumption which too easily panders to the complacency of modern man, who like Rousseau himself, is willing to be relieved of the effort needed to undertake that slow and painful attempt at the clarification of what is involved in human existence which is what education

[1] *Emile*, p. 49.

at its best implies. An apposite comparison is with a man like Newman, whose dogmatism, in the modern view, appears to contrast unfavourably with the advocate of the Inner Light. Yet Newman is content to exist within a system which assumes man's essential imperfection, and he therefore stresses the painful effort necessary to bring him to even a reasonable degree of enlightenment; for, as Newman appreciated, there is '. . . no true culture without acquirements, and philosophy presupposes knowledge. It requires a great deal of reading or a wide range of information, to warrant us putting forth our opinions on any serious subject' (*The Idea of a University*). Newman remains the true advocate of civilization; Rousseau's educational ideas involve a regression to simpler modes of living. Behind the apparent humility of 'negative' education there is a certain complacency of ignorance, a lack of patience before the careful unravelling of what human knowledge has so carefully built up.[1]

What Rousseau has done for education has rightfully had its meed of praise; he is capable of much acute observation and the revolution of approach he instigated has conferred considerable benefits on education. At the same time, in criticizing him, one must not blame him for failing to observe what only half a century of patient child study has revealed. Nevertheless, near contemporaries, like Wordsworth and Coleridge, achieved a deeper insight; and Rousseau must take some of the blame for errors of observation because such errors are inherent in the mental immaturities of the man and are not essentially in the inadequacies of the time. As John Stuart Mill pointed out, no one's synthesis can comprise more than the elements of his analysis; and Rousseau's understanding of life would appear to contain some considerable gaps.

1953

[1] Sir Isaiah Berlin has called Rousseau the 'first militant lowbrow in history' during a Third Programme broadcast.

Freedom in Education

There are various ways in which it is possible to discuss the subject of freedom in education. I could, for instance, examine the freedom enjoyed by individual headmasters and staffs of schools, under the local authority system, to run their schools as they like, to frame their own syllabuses, etc., in contrast to the restrictive systems which are encountered in certain continental countries; or I could write about the autonomy of the individual teacher in the classroom *vis-à-vis* the headmaster and the inspectorate. But in fact I want to restrict my comments to the sort of freedom which has arisen in the classroom as between the children and the teacher, the sort of freedom which has, for instance, affected in some cases what is taught and has certainly affected the way in which the teaching is carried on. At the same time, it is important to realize that the sort of freedom I shall be writing about has only really affected a quite small proportion of our local authority schools; those which have been most influenced are the infant schools, and those which have been least, the grammar schools.

First of all, I want to consider, briefly, one of the historical influences which has led to this new 'freedom' in the classroom. In doing so I shall be considering a shift in our attitude to knowledge which has brought about both a change in the sorts of things which are today studied in school and, even more interestingly, has profoundly altered our attitude towards method, the way in which learning is to be encouraged. Indeed, one of the classic expressions of the new spirit is itself a *Discourse on the Method of rightly conducting the Reason and seeking Truth in the Sciences.*

For the great change in the attitude to knowledge which we associate with the names of Descartes, Bacon and Locke, was in part responsible for the development of modern ideas in education. The main tradition of medieval learning regarded knowlege as something to be deduced from certain *a priori* principles and axioms, principles derived from Aristotle or the Bible or, sometimes, the Christian Fathers. It was, that is to say, essentially authoritarian. Even a Renaissance thinker like Erasmus could assert: '. . . within these two literatures [those of Latin and Greek] is contained all the knowledge which we recognize as of vital importance to mankind.' At the beginning of the seventeenth century Bacon vehemently rejected the 'degenerate learning' of the schoolmen, whose wits, 'being shut up in the cells of a few authors (chiefly Aristotle their dictator) . . . did out of no great quantity of matter and infinite agitation of wit spin out unto us those laborious webs of learning which are extant in their books'. Moreover, Descartes wrote in French 'in preference to Latin which is that of my preceptors . . . because I expect that those who make use of their unprejudiced reason will be better judges of my opinions than those who give heed to the writings of the ancients only'. 'Unprejudiced reason' . . . the 'prejudices', that is to say, the unwarranted assumptions, which in Descartes's view inhibited all advance of true knowledge, sprang from the study of false philosophies and ready-made opinions imbibed from childhood. Error, then, was often the offspring of a false tradition; there is a powerful anti-historical element in Cartesian thought.

The 'new' thinkers of the seventeenth century, of course, had their own 'authorities'. Descartes advocated mathematics as the key to knowledge. The development of mathematical procedures was, in fact, Descartes's legacy to the progress of the new scientific method; for it is the new scientific learning which replaced the old authoritarian *a priori* knowledge of former times. The contribution of Bacon and of Locke—particularly Locke—lay in their emphasis on the importance of sense experience: 'Whence (asks Locke) comes [the mind] by that vast store which the busy and boundless fancy of man has painted on it with an almost endless variety? Whence has it all the *materials* of reason and knowledge? To this I answer in one word, from *EXPERIENCE*. In that all our knowledge is founded; and from that it ultimately derives itself.' And the two sources of experience were 'SENSATION and REFLECTION'. By 'sensation' Locke, of course, meant sense experience.

Now, with the mention of sense experience, something of the purpose of this historical introduction will, I hope, become evident. For, in the development of 'progressive' ideas in education, of those ideas, that is to say, which have played so significant a part in freeing the child, the importance of the role assumed by sense experience can hardly be over-stressed. From the seventeenth century onwards, through Rousseau, Pestalozzi, and Froebel, down to our own day of John Dewey, Susan Isaacs and of the practice of the modern infant school, the importance of direct, first-hand experience through the senses has been stressed over and over again as the proper means through which educational advance can be achieved. Here, for instance, are two extracts, one from Rousseau and one from Susan Isaacs: it is not, at first glance, easy to tell which is which:

'It is by walking and stretching and touching that the words "far" and "near", "large" and "small" gain their meaning.... To find out for oneself, to watch and repeat and watch again, for example, the way water makes a channel for itself through sand, the way one's toy boat turns over when caught in the swift current of the stream, or the way one moves faster or slower if one has a sliding board inclined more steeply or less—these are the experiences which give reality to the later study of "physics" and "mechanics" in which we shall want our children to be interested and to do well'.

'He wants to touch and handle everything; do not check these movements which teach him invaluable lessons. Thus he learns to perceive the heat, cold, hardness, softness, weight, or lightness of bodies, to judge their size and shape and all their physical properties, by looking, feeling, listening, and, above all, by comparing sight and touch, by judging with the eye what sensation they would cause to his hand.'

The sort of approach which these two educationists, writing at very different periods, are advocating is, in essence, a scientific one. Long before science was in any organized way being taught in our schools—though eighteenth-century 'progressive' thinkers like Edgeworth and David Williams were in fact introducing their pupils to simple physical, mechanical and chemical experiments—the *approach* to learning advocated by 'progressives' was basically scientific. The changed attitude to knowledge, then, which stemmed from those seventeenth-century thinkers I have mentioned, has involved a profound difference in the way in which, if we are progressively minded, we ask children to approach the world. For instance, it is, I think, too little recognized that the type of education which, basically, Rousseau wishes the child Emile to have is a scientific one; he wishes to encourage Emile to look at the world in a certain sort of way; he wants him, that is, to correlate phenomena in a manner characteristic of, at least, the earlier type of scientist. John Dewey, also, one of our most educationally important influences today, is deeply imbued with the spirit of the scientist. His educational ideas are very closely associated with the philosophy of pragmatism and such a philosophy springs from a conception of scientific method. The central tenet of this philosophy, in Dewey's own words, is that the 'hypothesis [note the scientific terminology] that works is the true one'. And Dewey looks upon human experience as providing data for modification and control: 'It is', he states, 'material to act upon so as to transform it into new objects which better answer our needs.' Experience is to be in a continual state of reconstruction —Dewey denies the presence of any absolute values. As an admirer of Francis Bacon, he also urges that knowledge is power; and he repudiates the 'authority', as we might call it, of the past.

Life, then, to Dewey presents problems which we recognize; on the data presented we build up a hypothesis as to the correct mode of action; and we test that hypothesis in action. If our problem is solved, we have discovered truth; if not, we must re-frame our hypothesis. Value lies in consequences.

Dewey's world, like that of the earlier scientist, is very much that of practical activity. He believes that 'scientific inquiry always starts from things of the environment experienced in our everyday life, with things we see, handle, use, enjoy and suffer from'. In the same way, Emile was to learn facts which 'are within his reach by experiment, and [to] discover the rest by induction'.

Thus the child was—and is—to be placed in the same sort of position as the early scientist. Such a view of the process of education involves a standpoint which is essentially anti-dogmatic even if fragmentary. Implicit is an element of freedom of choice, of personal discovery; it is not knowledge accepted on authority but through individual effort. Even if one admits that the view of scientific method is an out-of-date one, recalling the romantic efforts of the earliest investigators rather than the disciplined and restricted attention of the modern scientist, building on the efforts of his predecessors, it is still worth recalling that scientific knowledge at any level retains an element of the hypothetical and the 'democratic'; hypothetical because in the last resort all science is based on hypotheses, and 'democratic' in the sense that all scientific knowledge is publicly inspectable. It does not, that is to say, depend on the *a priori*, the axiomatic—except in the most general sense, that the world constitutes an order, for instance—or on the inborn innate understanding. Hence, the scientific revolution has done as much as anything to free the child from the tyranny of the pre-accepted and the authoritatively laid down. The cry of 'experience'—witness the famous words of the Primary School report: '... the curriculum is to be thought of in terms of activity and experience rather than of knowledge to be acquired and facts to be stored'—stems from Locke's denial of innate ideas and his stress on 'EXPERIENCE—SENSATION and REFLECTION'.

For in the providing of this experience—I am quoting again from Susan Issacs: 'The physical setting and the educational technique alike were designed to call out the children's activity, rather than the teacher's. The function of the teachers was to stand by, ready to make suggestions when these seemed appropriate, but mainly to follow the spontaneous interests of the children, and to foster their inquiries, experiments, and discoveries, in whatever direction these might take.' (Note the scientific use of the word 'experiment'—the children experiment with their environment while, to some extent at least, the teachers experiment with the children.) Hence it can be urged that the scientific revolution which originally stems from the thirteenth-century work of Roger Bacon and Grosseteste, but which only becomes the predominating influence and tradition in the seventeenth century, has done as much as anything to create the psychological and epistemological conditions within which 'freedom' in general—and 'freedom in education' in particular—comes to be felt as a problem. Of course, there were other powerful influences at work—for example the development of Protestantism; the relationship with God becomes a personal one instead of needing the interposition of a Church. Furthermore there has been the breakdown of an economic system based on hierachy and status, and the development of capitalistic enterprise on the 'freedom of the market', culminating in the *laissez-faire* policy of nineteenth-century liberalism. There has been the social and political development of democracy, particularly of the egalitarian streak which is today crying out for the reorganization of the secondary schools; and anyone who is acquainted with the work of John Dewey is not likely to make the mistake of underestimating the part played by such socio-political ideas even in the limited sphere of the classroom. The project method, for instance, is not only an educational technique; it is a social one as well. If, then, I have concentrated on the part played by science, it is because from an educational standpoint a shift in ideas about knowledge seems to be more immediately relevant. Furthermore, the interest in the laws of nature which scientific investigation stimulated led to the formulation of that conception of freedom in education which held that freedom results from conformity with the natural law of development inherent in the growth of the individual. At the same time, the development of science represents only one strand, though a very important one, in the texture of events which has produced the modern problem of freedom. I adduce it because I agree with Erich Fromm, when, in his *Fear of Freedom*, he urges that 'any understanding of freedom in modern society must start with that period in which the foundations of modern culture were laid'. A major characteristic of that period lay in the development of the scientific attitude.

But now I want to point to one of our basic dilemmas in considering the problem of freedom, in education as in politics or elsewhere. In the last quotation I made from Susan Isaacs she refers to the function of the teachers as being 'mainly to follow the spontaneous interests of the children'. The concern for spontaneity, which ten years ago attracted a good deal of attention in educational circles, springs from a romantic, individualistic view of the personality. Non-interference by the teacher is justified on the grounds that the child is a being with a separate entity, an inner life essentially different from that of the adult, a view which became widely advertised about the time of Rousseau: 'Childhood has its own ways of seeing, thinking and feeling; nothing is more foolish than to try and substitute our ways.' Combine this with the other Rousseauesque dictum: 'Let us lay it down as an incontrovertible rule that the first impulses of nature are always right,' and something of the ideological basis of the belief in 'spontaneity' is revealed. Implicit, then, in this emphasis on the virtues of spontaneity is a conception of freedom which regards freedom negatively, i.e. as an absence of restraint. And one of the important ways in which children have achieved freedom in our time lies precisely in this lifting of many of the restraints of adult authority—restraints which in the field of education can be described as both academic and moral. Academically it is possible to see the results of this in Susan Isaac's view of her aims in the passage I have just quoted; and, I might add, in the notion of choice of activities, a choice which often faces the child in the significantly named though now slightly démodé 'Free Activity' school. A reluctance to embark on moral judgments sprang from a belief in the dangers of an over-stimulation of the super-ego, and can again be noted in Susan Isaacs's comment that at her school she 'never used general categories such as "naughty", "good" or "horrid".'

Adults then, parents and teachers, have abdicated a good deal of the sort of authority, and abandoned many of the restraints which not so long ago were normally accepted as part of the usual pattern of bringing up children. By such abandonment of restraints it is thought that the children will be helped to develop both personally and academically. They will be helped personally because their 'rights' as self-subsistent entities are recognized; they are accorded the right to develop in accordance with their own individual natures and not in accordance with a pattern of behaviour laid down from above; and they are helped academically because their own individual interests and aptitudes are recognized as important factors in any process of learning they are asked to undergo.

Yet, if we look a little more carefully at the sentence from Rousseau just quoted, we shall note that, despite all superficial appearances to the contrary, a constraint is mentioned: '. . . the first impulses of nature are always right.' At first sight this would seem to allow any and every impulse that the child would wish to indulge in. It is only when we read the work as a whole that the profound significance of that saving phrase 'of nature' can be realized. Implicit, indeed, in all Rousseau's advocacy of 'freedom' for the child is the appeal to a *law* of development in some sense implicit in the functioning of the *natural* world. Rousseau, indeed, in certain of his works, is concerned to shake off those shackles which he thinks restrict man's actions and which spring from the constraint imposed by social and political institutions, social custom and the like. But he invokes another 'authority', as it were, when he appeals to 'nature' (a highly complex and ambiguous concept, I would note in passing) as providing the necessary criteria for correct upbringing.[1]

[1] Whereas in education Rousseau is the great advocate of the release and freedom of the child *from* social restraints, in political matters he is the great advocate of the freedom of the individual *through* social restraints. Whereas,

Rousseau, then, conceived of the freedom of the child as springing from obedience to the laws of nature, for that is what, in effect, his appeal to the 'first impulses of nature' amounts to.[1] And certainly one of the things that Rousseau and others, such as Froebel, meant by this was that there was implicit in the child a propensity for development, for growth, which if not interfered with by human beings, would, 'spontaneously', in accordance with 'natural law', promote right development, the flowering of the 'real self'. For instance, on one occasion Rousseau says: 'Oh, man! live your own life and you will no longer be wretched. Keep to your appointed place in the order of nature and nothing can tear you from it. Do not kick against the stern law of necessity. . . . Your freedom and your power extend as far and no farther than your natural strength.' And again, Rousseau speaks of the requirements for 'natural growth' in these terms: 'The mind should be left undisturbed [i.e. by human interference] till its faculties have developed.' The implication is that the faculties develop spontaneously without stimulation from the social environment.

Now the view of nature implicit in these quotations equates the development of man with that of other natural phenomena such as animals and plants. It is not that Rousseau does not recognize certain differences between man and the animals; it is simply that just as there is a certain way in which animals develop untrammelled by human interference, so there is a similar way, if only we could see it, in which human beings

in education, then, Rousseau is the great progenitor of the movement towards self-expression and individual freedom from social restraints, in politics he is the great progenitor, in the *Social Contract,* of what Professor J. L. Talmon calls 'Totalitarian Democracy', i.e. freedom for the individual through the abandonment of all centrifugal and individualistic egotistic desires through permanent submission to the general will.

[1] Though there are times when Rousseau speaks as if the freedom of the child sprang from its assumption of rationality, when 'freedom' involves the rational self-direction of the will, implying a harmony of desire and performance: 'That man is truly free who desires what he is able to perform, and does what he desires. This is my fundamental maxim. Apply it to childhood and all the rules of education spring from it.' Rousseau was a contradictory thinker.

develop. Thus, in inveighing against the custom of swaddling children, Rousseau appeals to the fact that 'we have not yet decided to swaddle our kittens and puppies; are they any the worse from this neglect?' It is for this reason that the 'plant metaphor' is so popular with thinkers of this type; by the 'plant metaphor' I mean that metaphor which is constantly being used to imply an analogy between the growth of children and the growth of a plant: 'We give room and time to young plants and animals, well knowing that then they will develop according to the laws inherent in them,' says Froebel, and proceeds to lament that we do not treat children in the same way: 'In dealing with objects of nature we often follow the right road, but go astray when we deal with men.' This notion of the need to allow the 'law inherent' in children adequate opportunity to develop leads Froebel to say (and his words have in slightly different terminology been many times echoed in recent years): '. . . the fundamental principles of education, instruction, and teaching, should be passive and protective, not directive and interfering.' The policy of not interfering with the child's 'spontaneity', with his interests and desires, permits him to develop 'naturally', then, in accordance with some principle of growth which will bring him in harmony with the laws of development inherent in the working-out of the universe.[1]

There is, however, implicit in such an appeal to natural law a serious error, an error the nature of which invalidates the arguments for freedom based on it. This error has been so admirably exposed by Professor C. D. Hardie in his invaluable little *Truth and Fallacy in Educational Theory* that I will content myself with quoting what he has to say about it: 'There is no doubt that there is some analogy between the laws governing the physical development of the child and the laws governing the development of a plant, and hence there is some justification for the view if applied to physical education. But the educationists who

[1] I believe that in the popular use of the word 'natural' when referring to children—and indeed in some versions not so popular, for example when some psychologists speak of the 'natural phases of development'—it is at least *in part* to some such tradition of thought that the speakers are by implication appealing.

hold this view are not generally very much concerned with physical education, and the view is certainly false if applied to mental education. For some of the laws that govern the mental changes which take place in a child are the laws of learning. Now although psychologists are not all agreed about the correct explanation of the various laws of learning, there is general agreement that there are three main types of learning: (*a*) the process of "conditioning", (*b*) learning by trial and error, and (*c*) learning by what the Gestalt psychologists have called "Insight". But the laws which have been found to hold for these three processes have no analogy at all with the laws which govern the interaction between a seed and its environment. Hence our original proposition, "a child's education ought to be such that it is free to develop according to the laws of its own nature", if interpreted in this way, is false; and therefore there is no justification for the view that a child should be educated "according to Nature" with this interpretation of such a phrase.'[1] At the same time, it must be admitted that these analogies drawn from 'nature' have not been without their uses. They have, for instance, served to draw attention to the fact that, as in physical growth so in mental growth children do go, roughly speaking, through certain stages of development, even if at slightly different times and in slightly different ways from child to child; moreover, they do possess an *inner* potentiality, even if it is not one strictly analogous to that of the germ of a seed.

I do not, then, conceive the 'true' freedom of the child as springing from any theory of 'natural' development, and therefore I do not accept the implication that all we need to do to achieve 'true' education is simply and exclusively to throw off those repressive interferences with the 'natural' development of the child's inner resources. At the same time, I would admit that freedom from certain specific restraints, definable in relation to individual children in particular terms, is probably a necessary precursor to the attainment of what I have in mind

[1] Another interesting analysis of what he terms the 'growth' metaphor is provided in Israel Scheffler's *The Language of Education*, pp. 49–50.

when I speak of 'true' freedom. For instance, the child who is going to develop a talent for painting or sculpture work probably needs to be free from the constant injunction from his mother to keep his hands clean. In other words, a certain element of 'freedom from' or 'negative freedom' is a necessary precursor to any kind of positive achievement; though at the same time it is vitally important that the particular freedoms from restraint should not be conceived in general or conventional terms, but should be examined in specific cases in relation to particular personalities, as individual moral decisions. It is as well to bear in mind that a restrictive system and the tension that it can create *may* involve a not unimportant element in achievement. The removal of all difficulties and stumbling blocks may not necessarily be releasing, paradoxical though this may seem.

Now I want to go on to consider what is meant by speaking of 'true' freedom. I have tried to point out that freedom from restraint is not a necessary *and* sufficient condition of 'true' freedom, though I have admitted that freedom from certain restraints may be a necessary precursor. And, in fact, though freedom is often loosely conceived of in this way, I know of no teachers who, although they may well make a great point of stressing the need for freedom from human constraints and unnecessary interference on the part of the adult, in fact follow their own injunctions on the matter to their logical conclusion. If we may take Rousseau as symptomatic of the vast majority of teachers of his way of thinking, we note that despite his belief that the source of all errors and evil springs from the grown-up world (children 'cannot possibly become rebellious, spiteful, untruthful, or greedy, unless the seeds of these vices are sown in their hearts'), in actual fact he time and time again urges the need for human intervention. For instance: 'While the child is still unconscious there is time to prepare his surroundings, so that nothing shall strike his eye but what is fit for his sight.' And again: 'His sense experiences are the raw material of thought; they should therefore be presented to him *in fitting order*.' All this quite obviously implies a carefully thought out human intervention, though of a rather more indirect kind than that normal in the schools of his own day, or in many of those of ours, for that matter. About the fact of this intervention, however, there is no possible room for doubt.

Thus when Rousseau asserts: 'When he only does what he wants, he will soon only do what he ought,' he himself recognizes the essential ambiguity of this notion of doing 'what he wants' by urging in the previous paragraph: 'No doubt he ought only to do what he wants, but he ought to want to do nothing but what you want him to do. He should never take a step you have not foreseen, nor utter a word you could not foretell.'[1] For the moment, however, I want to forget Rousseau, in order to examine his notion of 'doing what one wants' independently of his gloss on the matter. In other words, I propose to examine the proposition, 'when the child only does what he wants, he will only be doing what he ought'. I will omit the word 'soon' from Rousseau's exposition, because this only introduces an unnecessary complication into the situation.

Now, although I do not think any teacher has ever held this proposition in its purity (I suppose A. S. Neill gets as near to it as any), there are many who have flirted with the notion, even though they have ultimately withdrawn from the marriage ceremony. For this is the ultimate proposition of freedom from adult restraint. Moreover, it suggests that such 'freedom from' has positive results for the child: if you do not interfere he will come to do what he ought to do . . . surely a desirable state of affairs. Why, then, have so many teachers who have had sympathy with the idea of children doing what they want (surely a sign of freedom) never felt able to maintain such a proposition as this in its pure state? If we examine the dilemma involved for anyone who tried to accept it, we shall come to see why freedom from restraint for the child is insufficient, and it will help us to formulate that conception of 'true' freedom which I have been promising for so long.

The dilemma is, in fact, a logical one; for there is no logical

[1] Here, indeed, Rousseau stands as the progenitor of both liberal 'progressive' and totalitarian collectivist education in the same sentence!

or necessary connection between 'doing what one wants' and 'doing what one ought'. If I say that I am doing what I want, that is purely a statement of fact; if I say I am doing what I ought, that involves a moral judgment, which is not reducible to a statement of fact. One can put it another way by saying that, as a matter of common observation, there are many things which we want to do which we know, or at least have a good idea, we ought not to do. (For instance, we sometimes say: 'I'd like to murder him,' but we know we ought not to do so.) The fallacy is that noted by Hume in the eighteenth century and examined at length in the chapter on 'Fact and Value in Education'.[1]

My point is, again, that the educational situation is inescapably a moral one. For it always makes sense to ask not only, 'are these children doing what they want to do?', but also to ask, 'are these children doing what they ought to be doing?' Or again, 'is what these children want to be doing what they ought to be doing?' And the mere fact that such a question makes sense in itself is an indication that what they ought to be doing is not reducible simply to what they want to be doing.

It is for reasons of this sort that nearly all philosophers have found in absence of restraint ('doing as one likes' or 'wants') an insufficient view of what constitutes human freedom. For instance, doing as one wants may very well lead to interfere with somebody else's desire to do what he wants, which, in revenge, might lead him to interfere with what one wants to do. Hence the elementary principle that what one wants to do ought not to interfere with the freedom of others sprang up, and desire becomes tempered with morality. Hence, too, the development of the view that freedom springs, not from following the unrestraints of impulse and desire, but from allowing one's desires to be sifted by reason; another version of the same basic idea emerges from the belief that freedom springs from the observation of the moral law.

This view of 'rational freedom', as Mr. Maurice Cranston calls it in his admirable book, *Freedom: A New Analysis*, is one

[1] Chapter 5.

that springs out of a particular conception of human nature which sees man as very often the scene of a battleground between desire or appetite impelling to action and the rational will exercising a censorship over undesirable impulses. People who hold this view often look upon reason as the supreme characteristic of man; they consider that a life lived in rational terms (which are also in part moral terms) lays claim to being a good life.

Now this happens to be the tradition of human life to which I myself belong.[1] I do not mean to suggest that the idea of rational control has not been immensely complicated by the psychological discoveries of Freud and others; by the knowledge, in fact, that we are subject to blindnesses and rationalizations which interfere, unless we achieve self-knowledge, with the exercise of the rational faculties. What I do mean is that 'true' human freedom does not spring from the *unrestrained* indulgence of desires or impulses, though that does not mean that no desire or impulse should be allowed—it all depends on their nature. What the attainment of 'true' freedom involves is some measure of restraint; it is, in fact, something to be realized, not something to be accepted.

Now let me translate this into educational terms. I have already suggested that freedom from some restraints (their nature to be defined in particular contexts and cases) may well be a necessary precursor to the attainment of 'true' or rational freedom. I will now suggest that some of the criteria for learning which are nowadays suggested, such as 'enjoyment' and 'interest', are not, in themselves, necessary and sufficient arguments for pursuing any particular line of educational conduct. I am *not* saying that such criteria should be neglected or not taken into account; what I am suggesting is that they are not, in themselves, sufficient; it is still necessary to ask questions about the value of the exercise to be undertaken. And *one*

[1] Cf. my discussion of the implications of the rational on pp. 33–38. There is, I think, no real incompatibility between *this* tradition of living a life in rational terms and what I say there. I am merely concerned to define more fully the particular nature of the 'rational' I hold to; I prefer to call it an 'intelligence'.

(though only one) consideration which may well weigh with us in making up our minds about the value of an exercise lies in the fact that this particular exercise or piece of work may enable the child to accomplish or do something he or she has not been able to do before. (I say this is only *one* because, of course, it still makes sense to ask whether what can thus be accomplished is something of value.) The point that I am making is that learning, though it may well involve a form of control over centrifugal impulse, also, and paradoxically, serves to 'free' the individual child (I am assuming we have assessed his mental capacity to benefit—but, then, the vast majority of children are capable of *some* learning). Just, then, as social freedom springs out of the acceptance of the moral law, so the freedom to perform various skills and to make sense of the world around us so that we can move about it, springs from the acceptance of and submission to the authority inherent in the various bodies of human learning. And it is a fact of human experience that the 'subjects' within which, in the course of time, we learn to move with the greatest assurance and freedom are not necessarily those which we are at first most 'interested' by or 'enjoy'.

My conclusion is, then, that learning[1] matters; and that on its maintenance our 'true' freedom, at least as it concerns the teacher, rests. That is why I maintain that learning remains the most vital prerogative and task of our schools. Or, to put it another way, it is to the production of moral, not 'natural', man that educationists are dedicated.

1958

[1] By 'learning' I mean, of course, to indicate a wide range of disciplines and activities.

Fact and Value in Education

When we speak of someone's being educated, we may be referring to a more general or a more particularized notion of what it means to be educated. Thus, when we speak of 'being educated' in the sense in which we say that 'life educates', or in which John Dewey urges when he considers that 'Every . . . continuous experience or activity is educative and all education resides in having such experiences', we are employing the word in its broader sense. We are referring to the sum total of the experiences of all kinds which a person has had during his lifetime and which have made him what he is. It is this sense which is implicit in Helvetius's famous dictum: 'L'Education peut tout,' and his statement: 'l'éducation nous fait ce que nous sommes'.

But there are certain experiences among the sum total which we undergo which we often want to distinguish in a more particular sense; we often, that is, want to select some of our human experiences, and refer to these only as 'educative'; and often we want to do this when the experiences have been of particular value. Thus we might meet a fine person of some kind, and we might say: 'Even to be with him is an education'; and we would be implying that there was a peculiar value in the man's company, we learn something from his conversation or receive some intangible insight from his personality. Here, then, we would speak of 'being educated' in a more restricted sense, implying that, in some way, this particular experience was of more value than the general run of our 'continuous experiences'.

When we turn from the passive to the active consideration of what it means to educate someone, this element of selectivity, it seems to me, is always present. Certainly, it would be regarded as an unusual arrogance on our part if we said of all the intercourse we had with other people that we were educating them. Such a contention would seem to assign a peculiar importance to everything we said and a conscious decision on our part to exert a certain sort of influence over others. For, when we undertake to educate someone, we normally expect to bring about a change in that person's behaviour or understanding or a combination of the two. If we think of the human relationships—and to educate implies some sort of a relationship between educationist and educand—in which the concept 'education' would be applicable, we think of them essentially as those involving a conscious decision on the part of the educator to seek certain responses in the other. Thus, if one person is walking along the street, drops his umbrella and another person picks it up, hands it back and walks away, such relationship as is involved cannot in this sense be called educative. Moreover, if a group of friends meet together to indulge in social gossip and chit-chat, following the whim of the moment in choice of topic, we would not again in this sense say that any one of them was educating the others. But, if a group of friends meet together and find out from one of them how to play a game or discover how something works, then the person who was demonstrating would, in a fairly trivial sense of the word, be said to be educating the others. The basic element then would seem to be that one member of the group, otherwise the equal of the others, could do something or knew something which the others could not do or did not know, and took a decision, by some means or other, to pass on his knowledge. He might do it by instruction, by demonstration or by placing the others in a situation in which they could learn. At the end of the process—and education is an interactive process—the educands would know something or be able to do something they did not know or could not do before. And the educator in so far as he can be said to have been educating the group and not simply dropping casual information he had acquired which accidentally added to the knowledge or skill of the other, did so of conscious purpose.

Certainly, when we speak of education in a formal, socially structured situation, we imply that changes are to be brought about by conscious intent on the part of the educator, who has himself selected both what influences shall be brought to bear and how he shall proceed to make these influences effective. And the fact that this takes place in a social situation through some degree of human inter-relationship and that a process of selection among possible accomplishments has taken place means that notions of morality and value are relevant to education conceived in this way. The means by which the educator attains his ends and those ends themselves are subject, and have been subject throughout the ages, to discussion and consideration. Even where means are concerned, effectiveness is not the only criterion (though it may be an important one), should the means employed necessitate morally dubious procedures (such as recourse to severe physical punishment) on the part of the educator;[1] and where ends are involved the relevance of considerations of value should be obvious.

The question then arises as to the part played by fact in coming to decisions about aims and purposes, content and the like. Part, indeed, of the difficulty of investigating what is implicit in the process of education is that questions of fact and questions of value are likely to be closely interwoven. In view of the importance of not confusing the two, for clarity in thinking about education in general, I propose to attempt to elucidate the situation by examining the work of one of the most justly

[1] Cf. The discussion by Israel Scheffler on the concept of 'Teaching' in *The Language of Education:* 'Teaching may, to be sure, proceed by various methods, but some ways of getting people to do things are excluded from the standard range of the term "teaching". To teach, in the standard sense, is at some points at least to submit oneself to the understanding and independent judgment of the pupil, to his demand for reasons, to his sense of what constitutes an adequate explanation. To teach someone that such and such is the case is not merely to try to get him to believe it: deception, for example, is not a method or a mode of teaching' (p. 57). Dr. Scheffler's book should be referred to for an interesting discussion of the concept of 'teaching'.

celebrated of educational psychologists, that of the late Susan Isaacs. In this way I will hope to show how subtly intermingled the evaluative and the factual elements in education are likely to prove.

Attempts to define the status of education as that of a science have been frequent since the eighteenth century. Nearer our own time, for instance, Sir John Adams, having to his own satisfaction decided that 'by combination of the inter-dependent ideals of self-realization and many-sided interest' we could 'be at peace for a while with regard to the ultimate goal of education', welcomed the introduction of quantitative methods as the beginning of a process which would turn education into a true science.

The turning of education into a science, however, has proved a more stubborn task than Sir John seems to have foretold. For one thing, the framework of aims he thought to have established has not found universal favour; indeed, in view of their vagueness, a quality they share with many such expressions, this is hardly surprising. And this in itself would be sufficient, if not to falsify his expectations, at least immensely to complicate the task of arriving at an 'objective standard', as he calls it, in terms of which the scientific facts of education could be validated. For a great deal of the difficulty involved in establishing the psychological or social facts of the educational situation springs from the equivocal nature of many of those facts. Thus, many psychologists will dogmatize about the 'needs' of children without appreciating that in the expression of a 'need' there is usually involved a suppressed value judgment—that propositions about needs usually require to be rewritten in the form: 'if you consider so and so to be important, then the child needs such and such.' It exists, that is to say, in relation to certain assumed ends. Hence, to establish the fact, from observation, that children like bodily activity is not necessarily to assert their need for it in all contexts.

Susan Isaacs, unlike some psychologists, is, to some extent, aware of the problems of evaluation. Thus, in the first chapter of *Intellectual Growth in Young Children* (1930), she explicitly notes her attempt to present her evidence 'as free as possible from evaluations and interpretations'. Her records of the children's behaviour she terms 'direct and dispassionate observations', and appreciates that '*ideally*, *no* interpretations should appear in the records' (p. 1). At the same time, she notes, rightly, that 'the act of selection is itself an act of judgment' (p. 2); and, even when the data are presented statistically, which, in her view, tenders facts to the reader 'with minimal refraction', the initial act of selection still remains. She understands that 'by looking for particular answers to particular questions, we run the risk of missing other perhaps more significant facts which might transform our problem and make our previous questions idle' (p. 3); for the grouping of material divides as well as unites: 'we bring *a* and *b* together into *ab*; and *c* and *d* are built into *cd*. But it may be that the relations between *b* and *c*, or between *a* and *d* are in fact more significant and penetrating; and *ab* and *cd* divert us from *bc* and *ad*' (p. 5). She also makes clear the impossibility of showing what children are 'by nature', because she appreciates that the presence of adults inevitably produces an effect on the child's mind; behaviour, even at a very early age, is never uncomplicated by social experience and in this experience adults play a major part. Even when an adult is not present, 'the behaviour of children in spontaneous play will have some inherent reference to the parental images'. Even the 'adult who does not interfere cannot be for the child himself a neutral observer—he is a passive *parent*'. Hence, 'the children are psychologically oriented towards him as an adult. Their world hangs upon him and his slightest sign is full of meaning' (p. 9). Thus she concludes that, when adults combine the function of educator and observer, 'many allowances will have to be made in all our records for our own direct if involuntary effect upon the children's behaviour' (p. 10).

Hence, Susan Isaacs quite rightly notes that both in the concepts in terms of which she interprets the children's behaviour and through the presence of adults in the situations in which the data were collected, there were distorting influences at work. The main cause of her difficulties, indeed, is to be found where she had noted it—in her attempt to combine the roles both of observer and educator; but the difficulties inherent in such a situation are even more serious than she seems to have realized, though she deserves immense credit for having appreciated that there is a problem to be met.

A preliminary inkling of her deficiency of subtlety in interpretation can be gleaned from some remarks she makes regarding the nature of the children's reactions to the free verbal expression permitted in the social setting of the Malting House School. She states that, in an attempt to gain a more truthful account of what the children's real reactions to situations were, they 'were not checked or scolded for the free verbal expression of their opinions, or their feelings towards each other'. Thus, she considers, was yielded 'a far richer crop of evidence as to what these opinions and feelings were than could be gained under ordinary conditions' (p. 8). But a closer examination shows that what, in effect, was learned was an indication of how children might behave or speak under the particular social conditions of the Malting House School; and the assumption, which appears to lie behind her work, that they thus revealed feelings or attitudes which, usually unexpressed, would inevitably exist in any contemporary English environment, seems to me unjustified. Thus the data she collects can only be interpreted in relation to the complex of circumstances out of which they grew. For the particular conditions which prevailed there must inevitably have stimulated action and remarks which would not necessarily have occurred to a similar group of children under different circumstances. The nature of the relationship between 'real' feelings and expressed ones or overt behaviour, which incidentally has furnished so frequent a theme in romantic writings, provides a more complex problem than, with all her acuteness, Susan Isaacs seems to consider. Thus, under 'free' conditions, a child may call one of his parents or some other adult a 'silly fool';[1] the assumption then might be that this is an expression of the child's 'true' feelings which, in

[1] At the Malting House School the children would call Mrs. Isaacs 'horrid', etc.

a more authoritative set-up, he would have had to suppress under a more 'seemly' expression. But this is not necessarily the case, though it may be so. For it is always possible that, where the relation between child and adult is of a sort different from that prevailing at the Cambridge school, the child may not be led even to *think* of the adult in such terms. Thus, one of the possible reasons for such behaviour on the part of the child, which would certainly not obtain in other circumstances, may be the irritation of helplessness which too 'free' an environment can provoke. Again, the type of assertiveness which such behaviour, as part of its 'meaning', involves may be stimulated rather than exhausted by the lack of inhibiting circumstances—as, indeed, Susan Isaacs found to be the case with bullying, which she had to forbid. Hence, it is not reasonable to assume that an environment such as prevailed at the school necessarily reveals the 'true' feelings of children in general, for the environment (comprising people and things) itself plays a part in creating those feelings through the dynamic interaction which inevitably exists between child and circumstances.

In other words, all social situations, even the 'free-est', have a tendency to evoke certain classes of response which are inherent in the conditions of their existence; and the assumption which seems to lie behind much of Susan Isaacs's exposition, that in verbally 'free' conditions we obtain a truer insight into child 'nature' than is possible under more conventional arrangements, is not justified. A more stringent application of her own appreciation of the distorting influence of the presence of an adult and of the stressed need to consider the '*whole situation* which affects the child' (*Social Development*, p. 7) in understanding reactions might have enabled her to see this. Her error seems to lie in her having asserted a too static conception of human personality, to have fallen into the romantic fallacy of positing a too rigid dichotomy between man and society, as if man had an inherent nature, more or less of which showed itself in accordance with the 'freedom' of the conditions within which he existed. Thus, though it is necessary to stress (since human personality is always unique) that no man ever completely surrenders that which it is convenient to call his 'individuality' to the social circumstances within which he lives, at the same time that 'individuality' is always affected, in some measure, by the particular social grouping and its dynamics to which he belongs. All, then, she would be justified in claiming is that in relation to a particular set of circumstances—and rather eccentric circumstances at that—stimulated, and, in some measure at least, controlled by herself and her staff, a particular set of children demonstrated certain characteristics and showed certain 'feelings'.

From this something of the extreme subtlety involved in the assumption of the dual role of educator and observer can be gathered. For, as observer, she should stand apart as a neutral, to record objectively, and as fully as possible, the dynamic interaction between the children's behaviour and the particular and precise environment within which they behave. But, as educator, she must inevitably take part as an active element in the situation; she is no longer spectator but participant. For the notion of educator implies at least the notion of relationship with the pupil, and she must therefore play an inescapable role in the evolving situation she is seeking to interpret. Now, to a considerable extent, as I have made clear, she understood this situation; but she does not provide—and, indeed, in the nature of the case, can hardly be expected to provide—much concrete analysis to indicate the extent to which she considered her role of educator had interfered with the objectivity of her findings.

This can perhaps best be seen in her conception of what she wanted the children to learn, in the sense that among her desiderata there were undoubtedly certain sorts of knowledge of a cognitive variety which she considered it desirable for the children to acquire. Indeed, she makes it very clear that she had some very specific *educational* aims (in this cognitive sense) for her school. Thus she was concerned to create a certain sort of environment; and she speaks of that environment as affording a 'richer, more varied and more immediate experience of the social and physical worlds' (*Intellectual Development*, p. 12) than is to be found in more ordinary schools. 'More varied' may be accepted as on the whole factual, relating to the numerical quantity of experiences possible; but 'richer' undoubtedly carries implications of value. And it is certainly true that throughout the rest of her books she regards the sorts of opportunities for learning afforded at the Malting House as inherently more valuable than those provided in other educational establishments. For the particular type of environment there provided was closely connected with her aims: 'The things provided for their [i.e. the children's] use, and the detailed ways . . . in which we responded to their various impulses, led the children to be much more generally active than they can be under ordinary conditions. This greater activity in all directions, originated, developed and sustained by the children themselves, was a definite part of our educational aim' (*Intellectual Growth*, p. 12). It is important to appreciate the implications of 'originated'; for it would be at most true to say that the children 'originated' the particular sorts of activity referred to under the stimulus of a carefully defined way of going about the business of the school in which the adults in charge inevitably played a major role. Admittedly, the environment 'evolved' during the life of the school; thus Mrs. Isaacs points out that, '. . . the main character of our technique was to meet the spontaneous enquiries of the children, as they were shown day by day, and to give them the means to following these enquiries out in sustained and progressive action. . . . We did not teach the children about these things, nor try to create an interest in them, nor introduce any experiments or apparatus until the need for them had actually arisen' (*Intellectual Growth*, p. 80). In this way, she speaks of following the 'spontaneous interests of the children'. At the same time, it must be allowed that the nature of her educational beliefs (which, as she makes clear in *Social Development*, were in the main derived from John Dewey) predisposed her initially to conceive of the school in a certain sort of way and also to pay a particular kind of attention to the children's behaviour. Hence, her employment of the term 'spontaneous', as usual in this sort of context, is unfortunate. For to the two factors I have just noted must inevitably be attributed some responsibility for influencing the nature of the activities engaged in by the children. The particular sort of tolerance and, indeed, encouragement which reigned for some types of inquiry, even the negative lack of stimuli in other directions, must remove much of the presumed importance to be attached to such manifestations of 'spontaneity'.[1] Again, the kinds of expectation created by the provision of apparatus to meet certain categories of question must have had a cumulative influence, have created a sort of momentum of attention to a particular way of interpreting the complex phenomena by which the child was surrounded.

Thus, it is essential to appreciate her findings in relation to those assumptions of importance, those values which pervaded the social atmosphere of the Malting House School; and to do this it is important to examine its physical make-up and its intellectual tone a little more closely.

What immediately strikes the reader is the fundamental distinction which seems to run all through the exposition between the 'real' world and a 'phantasy' one. This is very much the Freudian line: 'The records in this volume show how often and how readily the most active interest in things slips over into the dramatic play of father, mother and child; but they also help to

[1] As an example of what I mean, I will instance a sample chosen from the records of the children's biological interests: 'Frank and Duncan talked of digging the rabbit up—but Frank said, "It's not there—it's gone up to the sky." They began to dig, but tired of it, and ran off to something else. Later they came back, and dug again. Duncan, however, said "Don't bother—it's gone—it's up in the sky", and gave up digging. Mrs. I. therefore said, "Shall we see if it's there?" and also dug. They found the rabbit and were very interested to see it still there' (*Intellectual Growth*, 183). Mrs. Isaacs's intervention here seems to be quite overt and undoubtedly influences the children to a certain sort of attention in considering the problem of death. I make no comment on the *value* of this sort of attention; I merely wish to point to its stimulation by Mrs. Isaacs's question. Again, she asserts that the adults' part in the children's 'scientific' discussions was always 'restrained', yet she admits that 'our last appeal was always to fact and away from dogma'. She urges that she did not tell them what the facts *were*; but merely suggested: 'Did you look? Let's find out.' Nevertheless, it is obvious that such exhortations both indicate a particular mode of apprehension or slant of attention and circumscribe the world of discourse within which the solution is to be found.

show that their deeper sources do not prevent these interests from leading on to real experience, and from crystallizing out into forms of sustained enquiry, and delight in the actual process of discovery, which are at least anticipations of the genuine scientific spirit. The events of the real world are, indeed, often a joy to the child, as to us, just because they offer an escape from the pressure of phantasy' (*Intellectual Growth*, pp. 18–19). Again, a little later, she urges: 'We held one of our tasks as educators to be that of counteracting the dramatic tensions in the child's mind; and the only way to do this is to bring in the real world at every possible point. The way out from the world of phantasy is through the constant appeal to objective reality, to physical and social facts, and to interests and activities directed upon these' (Ibid., p. 33). What, then, is the constitution of this 'real world', of these physical and, in so far as they are relevant to her cognitive aims, social, facts, as she conceives them?

By and large, the physical world she has in mind is that which provides data for the scientist. In the concrete practice of the school, arising in part out of the apparatus provided, and in part out of the children's 'spontaneous' questions, she was mainly concerned to stimulate their intellectual life so as to lead them to correlate the phenomena by which they were surrounded in a way to which we accord the generic term 'scientific'. This interest in science was at once theoretical, in the sense that the children were to be helped to regard the events around them as manifestations of a certain causal sequence, and technical, in the sense that they were encouraged to investigate how certain objects were made or put together. Thus, in urging that the task of the school is 'to bring the world to him, in ways and at a pace fixed by his needs and interests', she remarks that, 'They are eager to watch and "find out" about all the concrete events of the home and the street: the structure and arrangement of the house, the drains and water-supply, the electric light, the gas-cooker and fire, the telephone, everything connected with cooking and cleaning, the street drains, road-making and mending, the shops, motor-cars and buses, the policeman's way of directing traffic, the railway station; the facts of their feeding and washing and digesting and excreting and growing, and the whole cycle of life in animals and plants and the human family' (Ibid., p. 17). In other words, the 'children's immediate and concrete world, the twentieth-century world . . . of motor-cars, engines, aeroplanes, gramophones and the wireless' (p. 22), is to form the material for much of their learning. This is further implied in the sorts of apparatus which were gradually supplied, comprising many varieties of constructive tools and material (e.g. paper, plasticine, paints, scissors, materials, carpenter's implements, bricks, pulley, etc.[1]) and scientific apparatus (various laboratory materials, animals for biological investigation, etc.). Thus, one at least of the quite ostensible and admitted aims of the school was to note the development in young children of the scientific way of regarding phenomena and to provide opportunities for its stimulation. And, in doing this, Susan Isaacs made an explicit contrast between the sorts of material on which she undoubtedly encouraged the children to employ themselves and what she rather vaguely refers to as the usual 'school subjects' [the influence of Dewey is patent here]: 'To us, the direct interests of the child in the concrete processes in the world around him seem far more significant in themselves, and as a medium of education, than knowledge of the traditional "subjects" of the schoolroom. In other words, we see no reason to let the school and its conventions stand between the child and real situations in the world' (Ibid., p. 21).[2]

Now, it is quite obvious that in the setting out of this account Susan Isaacs blurs the vital distinction to be observed between the factual and the evaluative element. Thus, there is little doubt that she succeeds in establishing the fact that, *given certain conditions*, the findings of other psychologists (notably in this case Piaget) concerning the possibilities of intellectual

[1] Some of this apparatus was, of course, used for various sorts of make-believe play and also for artistic expression.

[2] The use of the word 'real' in these contexts, invites close analysis. In what sense can the ordinary school subjects be regarded as not 'real'? Why is the outer physical world more 'real' than the inner world of emotions and desires?

development in young children, are mistaken.[1] The growth of the mental life of the child need not necessarily be marked by those well-defined stages that Piaget considered proven by his own researches. We can, therefore, accept her findings that it is *possible* for children younger than Piaget had shown to take a certain sort of objective interest in the world around them. But she does not prove, nor even provide any good rational arguments to support her view, that children *ought* to be stimulated to develop in this sort of way. She is content to urge, on unexamined grounds, that in some way these 'direct interests of the child in the concrete processes of the world around him *seem* far more significant in themselves, and as a medium of education, than knowledge of the traditional "subjects" of the school-room'. (Her italics.) And one can perhaps venture a guess that it was because to Susan Isaacs these interests of the children seemed significant in themselves, accorded, in fact, with her own private and assumed conceptions of value, that they also appeared significant as media of education. It may be urged that it was because of the 'interest' of the children, because their 'spontaneous questions' were directed in this way, that she, by implication at least, provides sufficient grounds for her choice. But I have already shown above certain grounds for doubting the true 'spontaneity' of these questions. Moreover, even if we were to allow that their questions were, in fact, spontaneous, and that their interests lay in this direction, would this provide adequate grounds for thinking that such interests, such spontaneous queries afforded a sufficient basis for an educative undertaking? It is obvious in the day-to-day handling of the children and of their social relationships, that certain of their 'interests', of their 'spontaneous behaviour', were checked. Bullying was stopped; there were 'definite limits set in certain directions by considerations of real bodily safety'; only one child at a time (to choose one from a number of prohibitions) was allowed to climb on the roof of the summer house; and this 'in spite of protests and many attempts to defy this prohibition' (ibid., p. 25), which would seem to suggest both 'interest' and

[1] She discusses Piaget's views at length in *Intellectual Growth*, Chapter III.

'spontaneous' desire. Again, there were certain requirements of hygiene (the washing of hands for meals, etc.), which, if necessary, were enforced by 'definite command'. And all this is quite in line with the opinions, expressed in *Social Development*, that the 'parents and the adults who make up his social world should represent [to the child] a stable and ordered world of values', and that 'there are times with every child when he needs to feel that he can be *made* to do things' (p. 421).

Thus, it is quite obvious that the psychological facts of 'interest' and 'spontaneous desire' are not the only criteria Susan Isaacs is prepared to apply in judging the social behaviour of young children; there would not therefore seem to be any *a priori* reason why they should be the sole accepted criteria in the field of mental development. The point is, of course, at least in part, that the assessment of socially undesirable behaviour is much easier to arrive at and much more obvious in its repercussions than is the discrimination necessary in the field of mental events.

But there is a further serious error—a logical one—implied in her exposition; and the appreciation of this really provides the crux of the matter. The basis of her error again appears to be a confusion which exists between the functions of educator and observer. As educator she is inevitably involved in the problem of values as I have indicated; even if she simply chooses to follow every whim which the children express (and, obviously, from what I have just quoted, this, in certain spheres, was certainly not the case), as educator she can only justify such behaviour on her part by making clear that that is the *best* way, out of the other possible choices open to her to perform her function. But, in fact, her aim is a more explicit and defined one than this. As we have already noted, she has a positive conception of the sort of knowledge which she considers it desirable for children to acquire—one of the 'real' world. We have noted something of the constitution of this 'world'. But in *Intellectual Development*, she posits a relationship between psychologist and educator which raises important issues: 'We have been content to apply our new psychological knowledge of *how* the child learns, in getting him to learn the old things. We have not used it to enrich our understanding of *what* he needs to learn, nor of what experiences the school should bring to him' (p. 21). Such a statement calls into question the whole problem of the psychologist's function in relation to the ends and aims of education.

Now, the psychologist is concerned with the scientific investigation into the working of the human mind. His job, that is to say, is to describe how the mind works, or is likely to work, in certain predetermined circumstances. He can, for instance, help us to discover how a child can best learn certain things, or whether a certain child, of particular age and ability, is able to apprehend such things. But it is not his function to say whether such a thing ought to be learnt, for such a decision involves a moral or a value judgment to which the psychological facts of the case, though appropriate as relevant considerations to be taken into account, do not necessarily provide the only, or even necessarily the deciding factor. The error, in overstepping her role, which Susan Isaacs commits, is one the extirpation of which has exercised so profound an influence on modern ethics; and it has been best expressed in a now notorious passage by Hume: 'In every system of morality which I have hitherto met with I have always remarked that the author proceeds for some time in the ordinary way of reasoning, and establishes the being of a God, or makes observations concerning human affairs; when of a sudden I am surprised to find, that instead of the usual copulations of propositions, *is* and *is not*, I meet with no proposition that is not connected with an *ought*, or an *ought not*. This change is imperceptible; but is, however, of the last consequence. For as this *ought* or *ought not* expresses some new relation or affirmation, it is necessary that it should be observed and explained; and at the same time that a reason should be given for what seems altogether inconceivable, how this new relation can be a deduction from others that are entirely different from it.' In other words, from the empirical fact that children are capable of learning certain things it does not logically follow that they *ought* to learn them. The psychological is a factual situation, the educative an evaluative or moral one;

the combination of the two, without a clear-sighted realization of what is implied, is almost invariably fraught with grave dangers, and discriminations between them, in the present state of the educational world, a matter of the most important consequence.

How one would set about deciding what children ought to learn is beyond the scope of this essay. One can merely urge that educational value judgments are matters for rational argument and that choices ought to be justified by good reasons; we are not, that is to say, abandoned to the position that preferences are questions simply of personal taste or express merely the emotions and persuasions or exhortations of the writer, as Professor C. D. Hardie seems to have thought in his otherwise important *Truth and Fallacy in Educational Theory.*[1]

It should be made clear, however, that among the good reasons will be such sociological or psychological facts as are relevant to the case; though, in view of the complexity of fact at our disposal, choice will have to be made, on grounds other than fact, as to the relative emphases to be laid on different areas of our understanding. Fact, by itself, is an insufficient base for a judgment of value; there is always an extra step involved, if only in the choice among the possible facts that appear related to the matter in hand. For such a choice will itself be based on a judgment of value.[2] Our social and psychological 'needs', for instance, can be shown to be multifarious; so it is not sufficient to educe the fact of 'need' as an imperative of action. Furthermore, differences of value assumption may sometimes present even the facts in a new light.

Thus, one of the motive forces behind the writing of this essay is a certain dissatisfaction with the values inherent in Susan Isaacs's purposes. A full exposition of disagreements would be

[1] Hardie was much influenced by C. L. Stevenson's 'emotive' conception of ethical judgments. This approach has come under strong, and to my mind convincing, criticism in recent years, cf. S. E. Toulmin, *The Place of Reason in Ethics*, iii.

[2] How judgments of value are arrived at or validated is a matter outside the scope of this essay. It belongs to the field of moral philosophy where it is the subject of much controversy.

matter for another supplementary essay; it is not essential to the main aim of this one. All I can hope to do, in the space available, is, by a single evocative indication, to map out certain of the grounds of disavowal.

In that great, though neglected, educational work, *Fantasia of the Unconscious*, D. H. Lawrence has this to say: 'A child will ask "why" often enough. But he more often asks why the sun shines, or why men have moustaches, or why grass is green, than anything sensible. Most of a child's questions are, and should be unanswerable. They are not questions at all. They are exclamations of wonder, they are *remarks*, half-sceptically addressed. When a child says, "Why is grass green?", he half implies, "Is it really green, or is it just taking me in?" And we solemnly begin to prate about chlorophyll.' This presents a very different *factual* account of what is implied by children's questions from that posited by Susan Isaacs, who sees in them demands for a certain sort of information; their different assumptions of value enable the two writers to present markedly different accounts of similar phenomena. What, of course, I intend by this brief allusion, is that the values of Lawrence shall be placed in juxtaposition to those of Mrs. Isaacs. The concrete working out would involve a lengthy process; all I can hope to have done is to have suggested a readjustment of focus. Though, in suggesting this readjustment, I do not mean to imply that Lawrence, any more than Susan Isaacs herself, has the whole truth.

1956.

Education and Society

We have recently become very conscious of what are termed the 'social responsibilities' of the educational system; and the view that the school should respond to vacillating social pressures is commonly taken for granted. Behind such formulations of the role of the school, lie particularized notions which are intended to affect not only the general ethos in terms of which schooling is carried on, but also to influence specific aspects of the educative process—aspects such as the teacher's view of his own function, the methods to be used, and so on. In view of the practical influence of these doctrines, it seems a matter of some moment that they should be subjected to detailed examination; and I propose to subject some of them to such an examination in this article. I shall, however, draw my examples from the great social theorists of education—men of the calibre of Mannheim, Durkheim and Dewey—rather than from ephemeral statements of social obligation and influence such as appear in the daily press or the educational weeklies.

(*a*)

First, what are some of the more general principles involved? The central argument, briefly, is that (*a*) our society is changing rapidly, and (*b*) changes in the curriculum (and elsewhere in the system) must keep pace with these social changes. Dewey expresses the situation admirably: '. . . our social life has undergone a radical change. If our education is to have any meaning for life, it must pass through an equally complete transformation.'

Behind such demands there are several assumptions. One is that there is a necessary connection between social ethos and educational system, so that, it is argued, as in the past changes in the one have been reflected in the other, the changes which have been brought about recently in the structure of our society demand that there should be a corresponding change in education; as Durkheim puts it: '. . . our pedagogic ideal is explained by our social structure. . . . The man whom education *should* realize in us is not the man such as nature has made him, but as the society wishes him to be; and it wishes him such as its internal economy calls for. . . . Every change of any importance in the organisation of a society results in a change of the same importance in the idea man makes of himself. . . . Thus, in the present as in the past, our pedagogical ideal is in every detail the work of society, It is society that draws for us the portrait of the kind of man we *should* be, and in this portrait all the peculiarities of its organisation come to be reflected' (*Education and Society*, pp. 122–3 (my italics)). I will examine this argument a little more fully.

We note, in Durkheim's exposition, the jump from a factual situation to an evaluation. The sociological facts are stated: all societies show this correlation between structure and education —when one changes the other does; and the conclusion is then drawn (the implication is in the italicized 'should') that therefore ours ought. But if all societies do, in fact, show this degree of correlation, how does it come about that we need to be persuaded to make it? It appears that it must happen automatically anyway. The suggestion that there may be, at the moment, an imbalance indicates that there is at least one society (ours) which does not bring about this close correlation. This is confirmed later when we are informed that our 'moral unity is not at all points what it should be. We are divided by divergent and even sometimes contradictory conceptions.' Or again, that 'Everyone recognises that [secondary education] cannot remain what it was in the past; but we do not see with the same clarity what it is to become. . . . To-day we lack any expression to characterise the objective that education in our *lycées* should pursue; this is because we see only rather confusedly what this objective should be' (p. 141). Obviously, then, a change in social structure does not automatically induce educational change; and, because of this, there would seem to be some opportunity for human choice in what educational changes are to take place. This Durkheim himself comes to admit when he goes on to exclaim, in his essay on 'Evolution and Role in Secondary Education', that such changes cannot be adequately brought about by administrative decree: 'One does not decree the ideal; it must be understood, liked, desired by all those who have the duty of realising it' (p. 142).

But there is, of course, the further point that, even if education, as a matter of fact, does often reflect the nature of the social system, it does not necessarily follow that it *ought* to do so; to assume so is once more to derive a judgment of value from a statement of fact.[1] There is actually no necessary correlation between change in social structure and change in social doctrine. As Mr. Hedley Bull points out in a recent number of *Inquiry*: 'Social doctrines are contradicted only by other social doctrines and not by circumstances . . . changes of circumstances do not invalidate moral principles; but they destroy the coherence of sets of moral principles by replacing situations in which it is possible to act consistently with all of them with situations in which it is necessary to choose between them.' (He instances, as an example, how the increasing humanization of social life, manifested in the moral desire to relieve suffering, may interfere with the moral imperative to avoid birth control.)

There are, moreover, further considerations of a more general nature. Because, as a matter of fact, certain changes take place in the social structure, the educator is not morally obliged to follow them unless he is persuaded, on grounds other than the *fact* of change, that these changes are for the good. The ethical proposition that all change is necessarily change in the direction of the good, is not one that human experience could in any way

[1] Cf. 'Fact and Value in Education', printed in this volume.

sustain. Therefore, the fact that social changes take place lays no obligation on the part of the educator to reflect these changes in his curriculum. Change does not necessarily imply progress; and some changes may be for the worse. This, of course, is a matter for individual value judgments in particular cases.

Hence it is important to regard with suspicion Mannheim's assertion that 'norms are themselves not absolute but change with the changing social order'.[1] As a statement of likely eventuality it commands a certain assent. This does, in reality, *tend* often to happen; but not invariably nor for everyone. The extent to which norms *ought* to change with the social order is a matter for particular judgments in particular cases, where the grounds on which the adaptation is made go beyond the simple assertion that the change has taken place in the social order. Hence the fact that a changed social order no longer 'needs' classical scholars to the extent to which it did up to a couple of hundred years ago is not *in itself* necessarily sufficient to justify the dropping of the study of Latin, whose retention may possibly be justified on quite other grounds; and, from the fact that Russian is becoming a socially important language, it does not *necessarily* follow that it should be taught in schools, though the fact may be adduced in its favour.

We must, then, be prepared to treat with some suspicion these educational demands which are made upon us in the name of social 'need', supposedly arising out of social change. The notion of 'need' always implies an element of evaluation when it is used to persuade to a choice. But there is a further consideration. It is necessary always to examine the concept 'change' when applied to human societies. To state that society changes is simply a shorthand way of indicating that certain specific changes take place at varying rates over certain lengths of time. Some social changes—for example in speed of transportation—take place very rapidly—that is to say, there are considerable changes over a short period of time; other changes —for example in fundamental moral or intellectual orientation

[1] K. Mannheim, *Diagnosis of our Time* (Kegan Paul, London, 1943), p. 74.

—take place very much more slowly; and certain basic problems —for instance, those which pose questions relating to right conduct—seem to exist in all societies at all times of which we have record. When people stress social change, they are frequently concerned only with comparatively superficial manifestations of change; the deepest problems remain—what I imply by 'deepest problems' should be sufficiently clear from the context. In view of the element of value involved in all educational decision, it is not unreasonable to expect educationists to pay some attention to the deeper 'needs' of their pupils—needs which in this case recur from generation to generation and do not change with every technical advance; so that if one finds that, say, Plato and Shakespeare are still important, it is because they raised questions or analysed states of mind which are relevant in the West, not to a particular phase of society but to the human condition as it is likely to be lived within the foreseeable future. Even without invoking a world of supra-sensible metaphysical reality, it is still possible to indicate some more or less permanent human problems which are not susceptible to changing fashion or increased technical efficiency—or are susceptible so slowly that this can be ignored. The answers we give may change slowly; some, at least, of the questions we ask do not.

At the opposite end to what might be termed the 'community service station' notion of the role of the school is that which stresses learning for its own sake. When we talk about learning for its own sake, we mean, among other things, I think, learning which offers no direct social reward, which does not fit one for a job, which serves no current end of social policy. It is good in itself, not an instrumental good—a means to an end. The learner learns, it may be, because of the intrinsic interest which the subject-matter has for him, apart from any thought as to whether such learning will make him a better citizen, etc. At the same time, it *is* extremely difficult to conceive of learning which has no social repercussions whatsoever; it has frequently been pointed out that the attempt to classify human actions into two categories—actions which concern only the agent and actions that concern others besides the agent—is impossible to maintain: 'No action, however intimate, is free from social consequences. No human being can say that what he is, still less what he does, affects no-one but himself.' (Quoted by J. C. Rees, 'A Re-Reading of Mill on Liberty,' *Political Studies*, Vol. VII, No. 2 (June 1960), p. 115.) At the very least, the activity of acquiring any intellectual discipline is likely to have some effect on the character of the person involved and is therefore bound, in slight degree at least, to affect his conduct. Indeed, I suspect that the discussion as to whether one should acquire learning for social utility (or 'need'), or 'for its own sake' is activated by a quarrel involving two views of what constitutes the good society. What readily becomes sinister about the emphasis on social utility is the narrow range, comparatively speaking, of the activities which are permitted to the members of the society involved. Often the injunction to recognize social 'need' is a bullying device to prevent other people from following interests of which we may disapprove or in which we may not be interested. That again is not to say that there are no learning activities of which it might be reasonable to disapprove —Fagin's school provides an admirable example; but each disapproval necessitates a specific investigation; and it must be recognized that from the *fact* that I cannot see the social utility of the particular sort of learning I am considering it does not logically follow that such learning is to be regarded as morally reprehensible.

(*b*)

We are also faced by suggestions concerning the social role of the teacher. Dewey expresses a certain view of that role: 'The teacher is not in the school to impose certain ideas or to form certain habits in the child, but is there as a member of the community to select the influences which shall affect the child and to assist him in properly responding to these influences' (John Dewey, *Education To-day*, p. 8). Dewey here points forward to a new conception of the teacher, a conception which has probably to some extent been influenced by a changed orientation in psychological studies; and the fairly recent interest in the functioning of primary groups, and the stress laid on group dynamics have helped to stimulate further the formulation of a new relationship within the class group. The teacher is no longer, in this view, to be regarded as an 'authority', the representative, so to speak, of 'objective truths';[1] in extreme cases he becomes little more than someone who registers consensus in group opinions. The ethical implications and presuppositions of this attitude have been recently examined by Mr. Adrian M. Dupuis, in an article in the *Harvard Educational Review*.[2] He begins by setting forth the aims of the people who hold this view of the teacher's function and then considers the implications of decisions reached on a group basis:

'... the major objective of education, at all levels (such people consider) should be social efficiency; i.e. school experiences should develop in students the skills and abilities necessary to interact with other individuals and groups in order to achieve social consensus. Realisation of this objective implies the necessity for training in group problem solving, which becomes the very heart of the educational process.

'What, then, is the nature of the group decisions? These conclusions arising from consensus are not considered right and better for all groups at all times but are at the best the means to intelligent action for the solution of the problem in hand. The teacher does not lead the student to the correct answer, for it is the group's prerogative to decide upon an answer. The implication is that there are no right and wrong answers, especially to normative problems, no right or wrong ways of doing things either in the classroom or in administrative affairs.' It is not difficult to see where such notions may have come from;

[1] I am aware that this characterization of the teaching curriculum begs the question of the relative status, as knowledge, of the different 'subjects'. This obviously varies along the subjective-objective continuum; but all make their impersonal demands in relation to their different natures—whatever degree of 'assent' (Newman's word) that nature may necessitate. Cf. L. A. Reid, *Ways of Knowledge and Experience* (Routledge, London, 1962), for a discussion of the problem.

[2] Summer, 1957, p. 210–11.

the current socio-political emphasis on the democratic group process, involving problem solving and decision-making, is particularly likely to be friendly to such views of the teacher; implied, too, is a view of the superiority of majority to minority opinion. Such extreme procedures as those analysed by Mr. Dupuis are not perhaps often met in schools in this country, apart from the more 'advanced' progressive schools; though ideas in the running of projects and phenomena such as school parliaments, which are sometimes encountered even in fairly orthodox schools, owe something to notions of this sort. Such views tend to historicism (the view that historical events are as fully determined by their antecedents as are physical events, and hence that historical prediction is possible) and ethical relativism; they grow out of, though, of course, they are not logically entailed by the metaphysical presupposition that 'all reality is in a state of flux'. A 'democratic' fluidity is implied.

These ethical and metaphysical presuppositions are commonly found among those who emphasize the notion of education as a 'social process'. The spectacle of social change induces an acceptance of flux as the ultimate reality of the world and a frequently accompanying scepticism concerning ethical absolutes. Thus Mannheim speaks of the socio-political realm as one in which everything is 'in the process of becoming';[1] he rejects an 'absolute permanent' synthetic view of the nature of reality (for such a view, he considers, would mean a 'relapse into the static world view of intellectualism') in favour of a 'dynamic' synthesis of different standpoints, one which is 'reformulated from time to time'. Because of the relevance of these theories of reality and truth to any discussion of the authority of the teacher—the teacher, that is, as the representative of 'truth', deriving his authority from the nature of his 'subject'—a fuller account of Mannheim's views is important. I would not wish to maintain, however, that Mannheim would support completely the conception of the teacher's function implicit in Mr. Dupuis's analysis; though Mannheim does provide some justification for the alleged superiority of group understanding, and

[1] K. Mannheim, *Ideology and Utopia* (Kegan Paul, London, 1936), p. 135.

he does reveal the source of the relativism implicit in such a view.

Mannheim posits two criteria of truth, criteria which I shall distinguish as those of Objectivity in cognition and Effectiveness in action. I will begin by discussing his notions of Objectivity and of the nature of objective reality. Truth, according to Mannheim, depends upon a correspondence between subjective utterance and the reality of the object. But, of course, he believes in the 'existential determination of knowledge'. Briefly, this implies that qualitative knowledge is in some measure socially determined by the social position of the knower—'qualitative' knowledge he counts as knowledge apart from quantifiable, scientific or mathematical knowledge. This necessitates the rejection of any absolutes: 'The view that holds that all cultural life is just an orientation towards objective values is just one more illustration of a typically modern rationalistic disregard for the basic irrational mechanisms which govern man's relation to his world. . . . There is no norm which can lay claim to formal validity and which can be abstracted as a constant universal formal element from its historically changing content.' Hence 'every point of view is particular to a social situation'; for 'We must realize once and for all that the meanings which make up our world are simply an historically determined and continuously developing structure in which man develops, and are in no sense absolute' (*Ideology and Utopia*, p. 76). The same notion is implied in his view of ethics: '. . . an ethical attitude is invalid if it is oriented with reference to norms, with which action in a given historical setting, even with the best of intentions, cannot comply. . . . A theory then is wrong if in a given practical situation it uses concepts and categories which, if taken seriously, would prevent man from adjusting himself to that historical stage' (*Ideology and Utopia*, p. 84).

Man, then, is unable to achieve absolute ethical truth or contemplate absolute reality. Furthermore, he must keep up to date. The assumptions are that, in the first place, Reality is Becoming, or, as Engels puts it, 'the world is not to be comprehended as a complex of ready-made things, but as a complex of processes'; furthermore, that Man is part of this process of becoming, and human nature results from the interaction of man and the world.[1] Action and knowledge, indeed, coalesce in purposive behaviour: 'Not purpose *in addition* to perception but purpose in perception itself reveals the qualitative richness of the world in certain fields. [There is the] phenomenonologically demonstrable fact that in these fields the activist genesis penetrates into the structure of the perspective and is not separable from it.' How, then, does man achieve any degree of *objectivity* of view-point? Mannheim's answer is that he does so through comprehensiveness, through that is, the synthesis of a wide variety of social view-points: 'Totality . . . is not an immediate and eternally valid vision of reality attributable only to a divine eye. It is not a self-contained and stable view. On the contary, a stable view implies both the assimilation and transcendence of the limitations of particular points of view. It represents the continuous process of the expansion of knowledge, and has as its goal not achievement of a super-temporally valid conclusion but the broadest possible extension of our horizon of vision' (*Ideology and Utopia*, p. 94). And, elsewhere, 'pre-eminence is given that perspective which gives evidence of the greatest comprehensiveness . . .'. Hence it is possible that group consensus, arising out of a more comprehensive

[1] The changed view-point of 'progressive' seventeenth- and eighteenth-century educationists *vis-à-vis* the authoritarian and literary learning of the medieval and Renaissance periods can be summed up in the oft-repeated tag—'Things, not words'. The change from the eighteenth to the nineteenth centuries and our own day could be summed up in the phrase—'Processes, not things'. Thus, to extend the quotation from Engels: 'The great basic thought that the world is not to be comprehended as a complex of ready-made *things*, but as a complex of *processes*, in which things apparently stable no less than their mind images in our heads, the concepts, go through an uninterrupted change of coming into being and passing away . . . has, especially since the time of Hegel . . . thoroughly permeated ordinary consciousness . . . (Hence) the demand for final solutions and eternal truths ceases once for all; one is always conscious of the necessary limitations of all acquired knowledge, of the fact that it is conditioned by the circumstances in which it was acquired.' ('Feuerbach and the End of Classical German Philosophy.') This links up with the increasing interest in biological and organic science and the growing tendency to think in dynamic rather than morphological terms in psychology. Dewey makes extensive use of words like 'process', 'growth', 'development', etc.

range of views, could prove superior to individual opinion.

Where action is concerned, Mannheim adopts the twin criteria of adjustment and fruitfulness, which meet in Efficiency: that is best which is best adjusted to the situation as it really exists, under the analysis of the synthetic view-point, and, at the same time, which gives the 'greatest fruitfulness in dealing with empirical materials'. As the becoming of the world is immanent in the historical process, accordance with such process provides the criterion of fruitfulness. As Maquet puts it: 'Efficiency and objectivity find their common origin in the historicity of the political view.'[1] It is implied, of course, that this immanent process constitutes progress; otherwise the ability to foresee and act in accordance with the emerging social situation could hardly be described in a value-loaded word like 'fruitfulness': historicist moral theory tends to optimism: 'This ability to reorient oneself anew to an ever newly forming constellation of factors constitutes the essential practical capacity of the type of mind which is constantly seeking orientation for action. To awaken this capacity, to keep it alert, and to make it effective with reference to the material at hand is the specific task of political education' (*Ideology and Utopia*, p. 157). Indeed, Mannheim's analysis of the sociology of knowledge implies that the very discovery about the nature of thought such a conception of knowledge involves represents progress through the possibility it affords of increased rationality: '. . . the sphere of the rationalisable and of the rationally controllable is always growing, while the sphere of the irrational becomes correspondingly narrower.' This is to be the fruit of an increasing appreciation of the existential determination of knowledge: 'Whenever we become aware of a determinant which has dominated us, we remove it from the realm of unconscious motivation into that of the controllable, calculable, and objectified' (*Ideology and Utopia*, p. 169). It is indeed arguable, paradoxically, that there is implicit in this analysis of the sociology of knowledge in *Ideology and Utopia* an ethical norm

[1] J. J. P. Maquet, *The Sociology of Knowledge, its Structure and its Relation to the Philosophy of Knowledge* (Beacon Press, 1951), p. 11.

in terms of the desirability of an ideal of absolute rationality.

The view that group consensus provides the best source of ethical truth, then, seems to rest on the assumption that group opinion transcends individual view-point, affording that comprehensiveness which permits a more objective synthesis; and this manifests itself, according to historicist moral theory, in action which accords with the evolving social situation. Some such explanation would be needed to defend Mr. Stuart Mason, for instance, when he explains why he decided to start the Leicestershire experiment: '. . . however ill or well founded it may be the whole notion of segregation is steadily tending to accord less and less with the mood of the times. The social conscience may be unduly squeamish, it could be eloquently argued it is misguided, but undoubtedly it is stirring. I think it is as irresistible as the tide. It is better to take it at the flood.' Some sociologists, too, hold the view that, ethically, their function is to discern the trend of society and to work with it. This provides the basis of many of their educational recommendations. But such 'historicist' views can be attacked on several grounds. They often conceal 'absolutes' which they resolutely deny; and they rest on the unwarranted assumption that change (the trend) is always progress—or, to put it another way, that what is, or is about to be, is logically related to what ought to be, which, we have seen, it is not. Furthermore, even if we allow Mannheim's analysis of the sociology of knowledge a limited validity, it is certainly possible that *some* homogeneous groups at least may well be more subject to the 'particularity of perspective' than might certain socially isolated individuals (Mannheim's élite of the intelligentsia) who are able to transcend conventional view-points. On the other hand, it may also be conceded that a socially heterogeneous group might on occasions achieve a synthesis of view-points which could transcend an individual outlook. My point in this context, however, is simply that there is no reason to assume that opinion derived from group consensus is *necessarily* superior to that of an individual—especially when the group consists of children and the individual is an adult.[1]

[1] The whole historicist position, of course, has been resolutely, and to my

The teacher remains the central figure in the classroom. Furthermore, the views of the majority are in no way *necessarily* superior to minority opinion.

I wish now to consider the conception of man implicit in the work of some of those who stress the social aspect of education; such a conception is likely to affect their view of the nature of the pupil and of the function of education. All theories of education involve some such view; as Professor Stuart Hampshire puts it: 'If most classifications of things, other than the disinterested classifications of science, have their grounds mainly in human powers and interests, the distinguishing of these powers and interests, and the understanding of their relation to each other, have an absolute priority in understanding the whole range of our thought and the structure of our vocabulary. For this reason it is possible to characterise philosophy itself as a search for a "definition of man", and to interpret the great philosophers of the past as each providing a different account of the powers essential to men' (*Thought and Action*, p. 232).

Social theorists of education usually conceive of man as wholly a part of the physical and social world (an 'animal'): nothing of him belongs to any transcendental sphere; and what he 'becomes' is 'determined' by the interaction between his individual nature and social forces. It is true that a main distinction between different social theorists lies in whether the end product is to be fitted into existing society or whether he is to become a denizen of a 'new' society. But they agree with Durkheim in repudiating the notion that there is '*one* human nature, the forms and properties of which are determinable once and for all',[1] a belief which Durkheim considered had subsumed the work of educational theorists before sociology taught us differently.

Hence the importance, in theories of this sort, of notions of adaptation: 'If . . . education has a collective function above all, if its object is to adapt the child to the social milieu in which he

mind, convincingly, attacked by K. R. Popper: *The Poverty of Historicism* (Routledge, London, 1961).

[1] E. Durkheim, *Education and Sociology* (Free Press, Illinois), p. 115.

is destined to live . . .' (the implication in the context is that this is so) (*Education and Sociology*). In their more extreme form, such views of adaptation seem to imply that the 'original' personality can be dissolved into a set of social attributes without significant remainder, so that possible conflict between man and his social environment may be met through such adaptation. This may lead to the belief that social changes may be brought about which will meet man's needs more fully, or that harmonious adjustment between individual desire and social reality may prove possible. As Philip Rieff has pointed out: 'In liberal psychology from Bentham to Dewey, social organisation, not instinct, has become the source of and the limitation upon the perfectibility of human nature' (*Freud, The Mind of the Moralist*). Hence the frequently expressed need to reform society, so that by continual readjustments it is hoped that it will one day be possible to live 'in uncomplicated adjustment to an uncomplicated world'.[1]

In any formation of a 'new' society, education, according to Mannheim (and Dewey) is to play a major role: '. . . recent tendencies in education . . . no longer aim at forming an ideal person in general, but a persona which will probably be needed in the next stage of social development . . . through these efforts, the entire person is to be remoulded so that by pursuing these new types of personality it will be possible to transform the social structure in its psychological dimensions' (*Man and Society*, p. 203). By these means, he considers, 'man can be transformed'—in this particular instance, man is to be made 'fit for a society whose mainsprings are not competition and natural conflict'. Then education becomes not only a matter of 'communication of skill, knowledge and technique' but also one of 'those *principia media* of character formation' (p. 203). It is instructive to consider how this transformation is to take place. It is, he considers, realistic to try to change a person within a 'dynamic environment, so that we can stimulate a change in his psychological reactions, conduct and ideas, with a continuous

[1] Quoted by Barbara Wootton, *Social Science and Social Pathology* (George Allen and Unwin, London, 1959), p. 330.

reference to the changing stimuli of the social background. Whenever a school is conceived of as an experimental community, this kind of planned transformation seems to be at work' (op. cit., pp. 204–5).

If, then, 'education is rightly understood only if we consider it as one of the techniques of influencing human behaviour and as one means of social control', it is necessary to formulate a 'common strategy with the social agencies outside the school'.[1] Mannheim died before the movement for comprehensive schooling in England had grown to any great extent. Nevertheless, he would have approved of two features of such schooling akin to his interests—planning and the controlled environment through which it is thought changes in human behaviour can be brought about.

Underlying, then, both Mannheim's and Durkheim's views is the notion that man's 'original' nature is highly 'plastic'—a notion which has received a good deal of support from fairly recent anthropological discoveries, with the realization that man is capable of adaptation to a wide variety of different culture patterns, dissolving his 'essential' being into a set of local social characteristics. Such theorists hold a dynamic not a static view of man's nature; Mannheim, for instance, considers that '. . . a static psychology which conceives of "man in general" on the basis of what man is to-day is on the wrong track' (*Man and Society*, p. 200). Man's nature is thus very much determined by the political society to which he happens to belong—the word 'determined' is Mannheim's own: 'There is no variation of the human mind in itself, but reasonably enough only a variation determined by the situation'—though he admits that 'there is, no doubt, a line beyond which innate hereditary traits and certain principles of social organization hold sway'—for man's nature, though plastic, is, he admits, not infinitely so. When speaking of the role of psychology in helping to bring about the necessary human transformation for a planned society, Mannheim indicates that what he has in mind is a social psychology: 'It will investigate how thought and

[1] K. Mannheim, *Diagnosis of our Time* (Kegan Paul, London, 1943), p. 74.

experience are formed by the social positions arising out of the social structure. With these observations as a beginning, it will be possible to mould personal intercourse in a more realistic way' (*Man and Society*, p. 202).

Both Mannheim and Durkheim agree, then, in denying any conception of man which posits an *essential* nature. To this extent they are environmentalists—they believe in the force of Nurture. And they would agree that sociological analysis is an essential prerequisite to the formulation of educational aims. Individual psychology needs in large measure to be replaced by sociology and social psychology.

This belief in the overwhelming force of circumstances in the development of the individual plays an important part in the educational thinking of our times. It is a major factor in Soviet educational policy; and, though it has not been pressed to such extremes in this country, most left-wing thinkers look to deleterious social conditions as the chief inhibiting agent in educational advancement. A belief in the equalizing force of similar social conditions lies behind the 'comprehensive' philosophy; and it has been shown that even the IQ, once thought to represent the native intelligence of the individual uncontaminated by family or environmental factors, is, in fact, to some degree affected by socio-cultural influences. Current concern for 'wastage' among working-class pupils is also influenced by the belief that the inhibiting influences are environmental.

There are, however, two important reservations to be made. Hereditary factors place considerable limitations on human adaptability. More important, the very power assigned to the environment should inhibit us from thinking that school education can bring about rapid reorientation. It is commonly admitted that the early years of childhood exercise a vital formative influence on later development; every child, by the time he gets to school, has already imbibed, consciously and unconsciously from his family background and neighbourhood, speech characteristics, emotional attributes, etc., which the relatively more superficial school environment, with its predominantly cognitive emphasis, can do little about except where unusual intellectual powers are in question. What can be changed most easily are the cognitive resources of the individual; what remain more impervious to alteration are the profounder emotional and unconscious aspects of the personality based on early experience. Human nature, because it always grows out of an historical context, is less plastic than our current environmentalists would like to think. Recent remarks on the failure of the comprehensive school to socialize its more difficult children will come as no surprise to those who bear this truth in mind.[1]

(*c*)

Finally, social theorists of education usually advocate certain differences in educational methodology, though the suggestion we shall examine is also characteristic of the 'progressive' approach in general. The fact that society seems to be changing so rapidly is thought to necessitate the development of flexibility of outlook in children rather than the acquiring of knowledge. As Dewey puts it: 'With the advent of democracy and modern industrial conditions, it is impossible to foretell definitely just what civilization will be twenty years from now. Hence it is impossible to prepare the child for any precise set of conditions. To prepare him for the future life means to give him command of himself; it means so to train him that he will have the full and ready use of all his capacities.' Hence the current emphasis on skills and problem solving rather than on the presentation of logically ordered information. The Herbartian approach involved a teacher-centred mode of education, where it was assumed that the main job of teacher was the orderly presentation of subject-matter, so that the scholar could acquire knowledge which already existed. Implicit in such a method is a view of education which conceives of it in terms of the handing on of an already existing culture, of the acquiring of ready-made

[1] The only person I know of who has really examined the possible implications of this is T. S. Eliot in *Notes Towards the Definition of Culture* (Faber and Faber, London, 1948). His book makes any further comment from me superfluous.

material, though made palatable, psychologically, by the skilled presentation of the teacher. The educative process here involves a building up, a gradual accretion of knowledge in carefully defined steps. The newer, socially oriented approach differs in two ways. In the first place, it conceives of learning in heuristic terms, so that the pupil acquires the skills which are inherent in the process of learning at least as much as the knowledge itself; to put it another way, he is learning *how* to learn as well as *what* to learn. But an essential part of this technique, which has characterized the whole approach to 'active' learning, is the situational setting in which the learning is to take place: Dewey considers

'—the only true education comes through the stimulation of the child's powers by the demands of the social situation in which he finds himself.

'—the child should be stimulated and controlled in his work through the life of the community.'

This approach is characteristic of Mannheim also: 'The essential changes in the methods of modern education spring from the discovery that the vital clue to the moulding of character and integration of personality lies in the mastery of the situation by the pupil. Only authoritarian teaching tries to develop isolated qualities, attitudes, and habits, and to instill ready-made knowledge so that the citizen may become evermore ready to respond to centralized command. Any education which aims at producing citizens who will be capable of independent judgment and spontaneous co-operation will train its pupils to respond to situations. The situation is the simplest context in which the child can be taught to use his own judgment and thus to face the elementary conflicts of everyday life' (*Man and Society*, p. 305). Here, indeed, there are two aspects involved. The young are helped to acquire knowledge in the traditional sense, but as a result of their own activity instead of through instruction by the teacher. Secondly, the element of control which is exercised in all learning situations comes, not from the teacher, but from the social situation itself: 'The basic control resides in the nature of the situations in which the young take part. In social situations the young have to refer their way of acting to what others are doing and make it fit in. This directs their action to a common result, and gives an understanding common to the participants. For all mean the same thing, even when performing different acts. This common understanding of the means and ends of action is the essence of social control. . . . To achieve this internal control through identity of interest and understanding is the business of education' (Dewey). In other words, the teacher is to exercise control indirectly through the sorts of social situations which he allows the child to explore, not through imposed lesson-material. This, of course, leads easily to the replacement of the teacher's disciplinary authority by group consensus, to which we have already referred. Furthermore, there is implicit in such views of the educational importance of situations a tendency to envisage the school as encompassing more aspects of the child's personality than are involved in the normal learning processes—Mannheim speaks of the 'moulding of character and integration of personality', phrases which conjure up notions related to the concept of the 'whole' child.

There are several points to be made here. It is by no means always clear in expositions of this type whether the situations involved are always to be social or whether they may also sometimes be 'physical' as well—as in scientific learning, for instance. Furthermore, the sorts of social situations involved may be of two kinds: social situations in which the learner is a participant —as in a group project—or situations of which he is simply an observer. Where the child is to learn as a participant, there are dangers that what may be induced is a conformism to accepted mores; a danger which Deweyism, for instance, has not always avoided.[1] Also, as it is arguable that a school is an institution which exists primarily for the acquiring of certain arts of learning—being the only institution in our society in which such learning can take place—an important criterion by which the usefulness of the situational approach can be judged is effective-

[1] Cf. my essay on 'John Dewey and Education', reprinted in *Education in an Industrial Society*.

ness. In so far as the situational approach is relevant to the *sort* of learning which takes place, encourages inquiry within that learning situation, so that it stimulates not only learning but the ability to learn, it should be encouraged; but in so far as the learning is not furthered by the social situational approach—in the study of certain sorts of literature, for instance—there is no reason to consider that this approach should be encouraged simply for its by-product of promoting social co-operation or some other social desideratum. Otherwise the curriculum may become distorted because those subjects open to the situational approach may get undue stress. This again, then, is a matter for specific judgments to be made in specific contexts; but they should always be made with full realization that the decisions we come to will very likely vary with the relative stress we place on different ends: whether, for instance, we rate a certain level of social efficiency above individual learning acquisitions.

I have tried to reveal the underlying implications of the arguments I have encountered and to assess their validity rather than simply to subject them to destructive criticism. In general, what needs to be stressed is the necessity for specific decisions in particular situations. It seems to me that some such investigation as I have tried to carry out is very necessary and that this detailed exposition related to specific problems, is the way to set about it. *General* attempts to assess the relation of education and society seem to me doomed to failure because of the complexity of the problems involved; we can only examine the situation piecemeal in relation to particularized claims and demands.

1963

Education, Social Justice and the Sociologists

There are two striking features of universal State education which, because of their obviousness, tend to go unremarked. One is that it is intended to lead to universal literacy, and thus constitutes an experiment in the development of cultural consciousness unique in the history of mankind. The other is that it sprang—as Arnold desired it to spring—out of the action of the State; it was the result of political acts—indeed, the provision of universal education was thought to be one of the first great acts of state collectivism. The political nature of state education has always been in some degree apparent. State education has, for instance, been subject to influence through the officers of the Board, the Inspectors; and administration by the local authorities has, to some extent, responded to local changes in politics. But the political nature of education has recently become more prominent, not only because of greater overt interference (the increasing tendency to subject educational provision to governmental investigation by committee and the subsequent repercussions on provision point to the increasing interest in education which the State is taking) but because the whole nature of our thinking about education is being very much influenced by notions of political justice, for it is largely in political terms that the more general notion of social justice is being interpreted. What was instituted in the latter years of the nineteenth century as a result of a complex of causes and motivations has gradually come to be represented in our public thinking by one great dominating political principle of abstract justice intended to secure a genuine 'equality of opportunity', both as an end in itself and as a means of developing all available talent to serve the further narrow end of economic development, the implications of which are largely political in nature. Social justice, which to Plato involved the total health of the State as its end, has, in our own day, come to be thought of in terms, largely, of the political principle of equality as part of the general collectivizing tendencies of our times.

The major effort of English education during the twentieth century, then, has been directed, not to the profound cultural implications of universal literacy and its repercussions on the health of the State but to problems concerned increasingly with fairness of provision, equality of opportunity, parity of esteem and the like. To view the child as a 'cultural' being would have been to see him in a context of the intellectual and emotional pressures not only of the home and neighbourhood, but also of the pervasive cultural influences of the wider environment (including particularly those of the mass media). Some of these would aid, some would certainly hinder, his capacity to interpret aright, intellectually and emotionally, the world he inhabited; and thus, correspondingly, they would aid and hinder his ability to move with confidence among the realities of that world. To see him as a 'political' unit is to view him more explicitly in the cognitive terms of an I.Q.[1] (a truly bureaucratic device of measurement) and to assume on this basis, his 'right' to pass over the various hurdles. Here, educational satisfaction tends to be seen much more in terms of 'ticket' collecting, of the 'right' to proceed to the next stage. The value of the educative experience in practice boils down to his ability to get into the right queue, the implication being that this is the major satisfaction to be derived from what is provided. If he achieves any intrinsic satisfaction out of his experience, well and good. But

[1] Or in relation to a limited number of intelligence and 'achievement' tests. These tests reinforce the cognitive orientation of the curriculum: 'It's not easy to capture the quality of the student's experience of a painting on an IBM card.' ('Knowledge, Knowing and the Visual Arts' by E. W. Eisner, *Harvard Educational Review*, Spring, 1963, p. 213).

the ultimate validation of the system tends to arise out of whether it affords 'chances' in narrowly vocational terms to the right people.

Indeed, assumed in much educational research (including that in the Robbins Report) are conceptions of educability which are hopelessly inadequate for the nature of the extrapolations based on them. But of this more anon.

Now, it is this narrowly political notion of social justice that an influential group of sociologists whose investigations have exerted a considerable influence on current thinking about education have, partly consciously, partly, through the pervasive emphasis of their work, unconsciously, fostered. It is altogether typical of the current climate of opinion, with its growing collectivist implications, that the sociologist should have recently risen to prominence. Ten or fifteen years ago, it was the psychologist who told us how we ought to manage our educational concerns. His assessment of what constituted a 'need' exercised a good deal of influence on at least the theoretical formulation of aim in education, particularly where young children were concerned. Today the educational sociologists (and, to some extent, the economists) have taken over; the nature of the problems they have chosen to investigate has focused attention on particular features of current educational provision. Perhaps their greatest triumph to date has been the Robbins Report, with its accumulated mass of sociological data, its vast presentation of objective statistical evidence, and its overt indication of political justice and economic motive.[1]

Mrs. Jean Floud, who is, perhaps, the most important of the modern educational sociologists—it is with her and her colleagues (especially Mr. A. H. Halsey) I shall be most concerned in this essay—has explained some of the current preoccupations of educational sociologists in an article published in *The Sociological Review Monograph*, No. 4, 'Sociology and Education'.

[1] The Robbins Report quite disgracefully neglects an analysis of current cultural dilemmas and fails to make clear how it conceives the function of higher education in an advanced industrial society. Cf. my Third Programme comment ('Educating Half Ourselves', *The Listener*, 19th March 1964).

Whereas the work of Mannheim and Durkheim was, in general, concerned about the problem of social integration in a society in which many of the primary agencies of socialization—home, church and neighbourhood—had broken down, the modern sociologist has become aware of 'the economic importance of education in an advanced industrial economy . . . [when education] is on the way of being converted into an increasingly rationalized system of mass instruction in the service of a modern labour force' (pp. 59–60). In this situation social justice manifests itself in the chance to participate in the struggle for higher-paid jobs requiring various sorts of professional qualifications. Hence, the current interest of the sociologist in the social determinants of educability, those factors which may inhibit working-class children of ability from gaining a higher education in current terms. The other focal point of interest—typically political in orientation—is 'our outmoded but by no means moribund class structure', which is threatened increasingly by educational developments, and which has in itself certain effects on the possibility of educability, so that the two lines of investigation involve a certain amount of common ground: 'In short, the relations of education to the class structure and of both to the national economy represent the most systematically and fruitfully cultivated tract of the whole field of the sociology of education in this country' (op. cit., p. 60).

It is rightly pointed out that the needs of the economy, particularly in their technological and scientific guises, do a great deal to shape the nature of the modern educational system; many of its characteristic features emerge out of the need to meet specific vocational demands for a variety of 'expertise': 'Modern industrial technology, based on the substitution of electrical and atomic for other forms of power, and introducing new and more intricate forms of the division of labour, transforms the scale of production, the economic setting of enterprise, and productive and social role of labour. It is dependent to an unprecedented extent on the results of scientific research, on the supply of skilled and responsible manpower, and consequently on the efficiency of the educational system.'[1] This educational system is characterized by specialized institutions of many types necessitated by the complex division of labour implied in a technologically advanced society, by prolongation of school life, by 'achievement' rather than 'ascription' as the basis of role allocation so that the system 'tends to become an elaborate apparatus for selection, training and testing of recruits to the occupational structure', and by the 'institutionalization of innovation' because of an emphasis on research which leads to 'perpetual change in the cultural basis of society'.[2] It is true that the system does not as yet work at full efficiency; it is urged that 'schools and universities function badly as selectors and promoters of talent', and 'for all the variety of structure and method in the educational systems of the industrial world, there is universal inefficiency in the prevention of "wasted" ability'. The reason for this lies partly in the fact that scholastic institutions have not fully adapted themselves to the 'tightening bond of schooling with occupation' nor were they designed to act as 'agencies of social justice' (and, here, one sees the close connection of this appreciation of the economic importance of education with the notion of justice). Education is still regarded in many parts of the world as the transmitter of an 'unchanging culture',[3] when it fulfils the symbolic function of confirming previously ascribed status, rather than itself having the functional value of being the means to social mobility—when it becomes a 'central *determinant* of the economic, political, social and cultural character of society'[4] (my italics).

Now, all this as a *description* of what, in some degree, is actually happening before our eyes, is extremely interesting, and commands a fair measure of assent. There seems little reason to doubt that, among a number of other events which are taking

[1] *Education, Economy and Society*, ed. Halsey, Floud and Anderson, p. 1.

[2] Summary of A. H. Halsey: 'The Sociology of Moral Education' in *Moral Education in a Changing Society*, ed. Niblett.

[3] Halsey, Floud and Anderson. Quotations taken from Introduction, pp. 5 and 6.

[4] *Current Sociology*, Vol. VII, No. 3, Floud and Halsey, 'The Sociology of Education', p. 169.

place in the world of education, the changes which Mrs. Floud and her colleagues are concerned to chronicle have their limited relevance. It is necessary to insist on the 'limited', not because the changes described are not, in terms of extent, important, but because of the danger lest the current prestige which sociology in general has acquired will blind people to the fact that the analysis outlined above remains a partial account only. For, indeed, the fear is lest what is essentially a *de*scriptive social analysis will turn into a *pre*scription, overtly or by implication; that, because an important trend in the social development of education has been revealed it will be thought desirable to implement this trend in terms of a 'realistic' appraisal of social possibilities in education, that economic 'realism' will become prescriptive justice. That this is, in fact, tending to happen I shall hope to demonstrate shortly. But, first, I want to consider the responsibilities of the sociologists themselves in going beyond their descriptive brief into the realm of value judgment.

In the first place, it is important to realize that the impulse to analyse the social role of education in our present society does not spring out of a desire simply to know, to add to our understanding. The field of the sociology of education is a wide one; and the concentration on particular problems suggests suppressed value judgments concerning importance and relevance.[1] The fact that there are comparatively few educational sociologists may mean that the problems they choose for investigation will obtain a priority of attention. Indeed, it is clear, from specific statements made by Mrs. Floud and her colleagues, that attention has been focused on certain problems because of a desire to implement further specific features of our current policy in educational provision. Thus, for instance, we are informed that *Social Class and Educational Opportunity* arose out of a desire to examine 'the ways in which the educational system affects the process of social selection. It is also hoped to throw

[1] There is of course nothing reprehensible in this—provided it is made quite clear. Weber recognized the necessity for prior judgments concerning relevance. But the fact that value assessments are implicit makes the work of sociologists open to attack on the nature of their priorities.

light on the problems of providing equality of opportunity in post-war English education.' In terms of the inadequate and denuded conception of human personality and educability implicit in the I.Q. measurement—the yardstick of ability employed, though checked against the results of selection tests—it is discovered in this investigation that 'Virtually the full quota of boys with the requisite minimum I.Q. from every class was admitted to grammar schools and the distribution of opportunity stands to-day in closer relationship to that ability (as measured by intelligence tests) than ever before (op. cit., p. 143). Nevertheless, it is urged that the problem of inequality persists at a more advanced level in the grammar school itself, when a number of children on the threshold of the Sixth Form appear to fail to fulfil their potential because of what are diagnosed as the environmental factors of home and school ethos. This phenomenon is summed up in the value-loaded phrase of the 'problem of social waste'.

Already certain questions raise themselves. The whole aim of the book has been, by revealing the current situation, to facilitate the further provision of educational opportunity in certain specific terms. Further, it is urged, in an essay on 'English Secondary Schools and the Supply of Labour'[1] that 'The Welfare State, on grounds both of political principal and of economic expediency, has made a renewed attack through its educational policy on the problem of securing a close relationship between ability and opportunity. The effect has met with a marked degree of success; but, as will be argued below, the organizational framework of English secondary education and the social assumptions which it reflects are such as to set arbitrary limits to the degree of vocational and social mobility which can be achieved' (p. 84). The profounder human consequences of this policy are not themselves subject to investigation, though they would form an interesting field of study, as other sociologists have realized.[2] Nor is the question of 'oppor-

[1] Reprinted in Halsey, Floud and Anderson, *Education, Economy and Society*.

[2] Notably Dr. F. Musgrove in *The Migratory Elite*. Dr. Musgrove shows some of the *human* consequences of the mobility promoted.

tunity for what?' here asked; it appears simply to be assumed that to give educational 'opportunity' is, in itself, a good thing, and that, if children do not proceed to realize what, on the basis largely of intelligence tests, is regarded as their potential, this is 'social waste'.[1] The adjective is significant; the danger in this type of writing is that the problem will be regarded from the point of view of the collectivity; the *human* aspect of the situation is rarely regarded or probed; or perhaps it is simply assumed that 'social' and 'human' ends are the same? Whereas it would be quite easy to show that, in the terms in which social needs currently appear, they are not. (What I mean by 'human' here will shortly be made more explicit.)

There are, then, a number of references which reveal something of the value priorities implied. I have already drawn attention to the degree to which the sociologists I am dealing with have been committed to 'the study of our outmoded but by no means moribund class structure' (*Monograph*, p. 60). Here, surely, the question arises as to whether it is legitimate for a social investigator to decide that a way of organizing society is 'outmoded', for this is a value-loaded word and only operates in relation to certain assumed ends; and it remains to decide whether there ends are, in themselves, good ones.[2] In fact, Mrs. Floud now makes explicit the aims behind much of the sociological investigation of education; and it will be noticed that justice (linked with equality) plays a prominent part: 'A desire for equality and justice and for economic efficiency, characteristically Fabian in its origins, has sustained a tradition of social investigation, which still flourishes, into the distribu-

[1] In fairness to Mrs. Floud, it should be pointed out that in a recent article, 'The Teacher in the Affluent Society', where she puts forward a view of the teacher as a '*crusader* in the suburb, dedicated to the war against mediocrity and to the search for excellence,' she does suggest that 'the tightening bond in modern economy between schooling and occupation' must be 'loosened before the teacher can play his redefined role'. The élitist implications in this view of the teacher do not seem to fit in altogether well with her conception of a communal culture examined below.

[2] A social theorist with a different set of priorities might regard a class structure in quite a different light. Cf. T. S. Eliot's diagnosis in *Notes Towards the Definition of Culture*.

tion of educational opportunity in relation to that of ability, its bearing on social mobility, or interchange between the classes, and its demographic and economic consequences' (*Monograph*, p. 60). It would be not unreasonable to accept this as a fair characterization of the impetus behind her own work; its left-wing implications are obvious enough, its acceptance of certain social desirabilities among a possible range. It is not, then, surprising to find her and Mr. Halsey suggesting that 'English secondary education should be reorganized along comprehensive lines'. They continue: 'There is indeed something to be said for the view that the common secondary school is best suited to the needs of a technological society—least likely to stand in the way of free vocational choice and movement, most likely to produce the maximum supply of skilled and responsible individuals particularly in the middle ranges of the occupational structure' (*Education, Economy and Society*, p. 89). Though here they add the rider: 'There are large questions with profound social and educational as well as economic implications, into which we cannot enter here,' Mrs. Floud elsewhere refers to our being 'deplorably encumbered, spiritually as well as materially by what I have heard described as "crumbling tripartism" '.

On one occasion, Mrs. Floud reveals something of her own larger conception of the good society. She points to an earlier tradition of social investigation concerned with the problem of social cohesion, of an integrated society, manifest in the works of Mannheim and Durkheim; this is a type of sociological concern which has recently been in abeyance at the behest of more narrowly technical emphases. She then goes on to give her own views on the problem of social integration, which she proceeds to analyse in its modern guise of a 'common culture'. She sees the problem of a common culture in the same terms as social theorists of the nineteenth century saw that of social consensus. After admitting the essentially divisive tendencies implicit in an advanced industrial society, she accepts the impossibility of a common culture, but goes on to advocate what she terms a 'communal culture'. This she calls 'a culture in principle acceptable to all and communally sustained, as against a minority culture fed and perpetuated by an elite' (*Monograph*, p. 63). This, of course, implies a significant repudiation of Mannheim's notion of consensus, for he approved the role of élites. But what else it implies is extremely obscure. It appears to depend on 'communication', which, in turn, depends on equality of opportunity so that everyone may be in a position to contribute and participate, though, apparently, unevenly. One thing that seems to be clear is that Mrs. Floud is against élites; the other is that the communal culture, whatever it is, is to be regarded as a good thing, as Mrs. Floud and her colleagues express their anxiety to get to grips with the fundamental problem which stands in the way of its fuller realization; the problem, as we have seen, of the '*social determinants of education*'.

In general, then, attention is concentrated where 'reform' is thought to be needed; underlying the descriptions there are certain prescriptions, admitted or implicit. Nor is this surprising when it is considered what, for instance, Mr. A. H. Halsey's conception of a moral education involves: 'The sociologist thinks of education as cultural transmission; he thinks of culture as that apparatus of adaptive devices of a non-genetic kind which enable man in society to adapt himself to his environment.'[1] And then, more revealingly still: 'For the sociologist the problem of moral education is the problem of social integration or consensus—the preparation of individuals for participation in social life and acceptance of social rules: in short the problems of role allocation and socialisation' (op. cit., p. 35). With such a view of moral education it is to be expected that at a time when economic motives are prominent 'education' should come to emphasize the training of skill groups to meet the needs of the economy and that it is largely in these terms that inequalities of selection should be revealed and social justice conceived. It is with this end in mind that we are urged to investigate the determinants of educability—without adequate realization of the tremendous complexities implicit in deciding

[1] A. H. Halsey, 'Sociology of Moral Education' in *Moral Education in a Changing Society*, ed. Niblett, p. 31.

the criteria of such educability. Questions concerning the desirability or otherwise of current social life are, in general, not raised: morality implies adaptation and participation.[2]

A most interesting piece of current sociological research would involve an examination of the current prestige of sociology (despite the very small numbers engaged) and of the prescriptive role sociologists (and economists) are actually playing in current theorizing about education. I shall say more about this shortly; but it is possible to conjecture that, at the moment, they are having things very much their own way because they have succeeded in introducing a note of hard realism in a field which has traditionally produced a fine crop of vague theorizing. 'Education' as studied in the universities has, by and large, emerged as a technology—a series of attempts under the heading of 'psychology', 'social psychology' and 'sociology' of education to work out a set of theoretical structures to facilitate the achievement of accepted or assumed ends. When attempts have been made to define educational values, they have usually only produced highly abstract formulations about social unity, Christian values, psychological 'need' and the like. The economist and the sociologist can introduce an air of precision, both in terms of demand and 'need', which fits in well with the planning proclivities of a large-scale bureaucratic state structure and, at the same time, satisfy current cravings for 'justice'. Against these requirements which can also carry with them the prestige implicit in their presentation as a 'national need' carping suggestions concerning the human inadequacy of projected changes come to wear an air of dilettante frivolity, of outmoded, if not yet moribund, humanistic preoccupation which are fundamentally irrelevant in the brave new world of the technological future. Yet the relevant consideration that technical and technological development in itself is simply an instrumentality, constitutes a means to an end and can in no way be regarded as an

[2] The exception to this is, as stated in a footnote above, Mrs. Floud's article on 'The Teacher in an Affluent Society'. Perhaps this article, a recent one, marks a deepening of her awareness of the specifically *educational* problems raised in our society.

end in itself demonstrates that concern for values is important, and that an education that concerns itself simply with a social justice whose only *raison d'être* is to further economic purposes—to afford 'chances' in these terms—would be an ineffectual education. To be strictly fair to Mrs. Floud, she sometimes implies a larger view of society and a conception of social harmony and consensus, which is to include abolition of élites and the coming of the communal culture, though she gives no indication as to what it is we are to share together or what it is we are to agree about. It remains little more than a gesture.

Nevertheless, the net effect of their work is to hasten a considerable change in our provision of higher education, for instance, which relates not only to quantity but, in some measure, to quality also. The process involved has been summed up by Mr. Halsey in an essay on 'The Changing Function of Universities': '. . . the function of universities as nurseries of élite groups is overlaid by their new function as a mass higher education service in an emergent technological society. "The community of the educated" similarly tends to disappear'[1] (*Education, Economy and Society*, p. 460). And, here, it should be noted from the 'trend report': 'It seems likely that when we are dealing with the mass educational services which are a feature of modern societies "instruction" looms larger than "education" in the broad sense of the term which is relevant to problems of personality formation or the transmission of cultural values' (*Current Sociology*, Vol. 7, No. 3). The profounder cultural implications of the movement themselves await sociological and socially psychological investigation.

My quarrel, indeed, is not with the need for social justice; but social justice as I conceive it demands a very different set of priorities in educational provision. It demands that every child shall, as a socio-cultural personality, have the right to that enlargement of his nature which a variety of educational provision can afford. And this implies much less pressure in the direction of a purely political provision of equal 'opportunity'

[1] In a recent article in *New Society*, Mr. Halsey regretted the numerical conservatism of the Robbins Report.

on the basis of an assumed set of priorities which accepts current valuations as to what is most desirable in educational 'opportunity' (i.e. the right to a grammar school education, the right to a university education as the most desirable rights). My views of social justice are, I would maintain, informed by a richer view of what constitutes society than that implicit in the sociologist's concern with class and opportunity. I want the schools to appreciate that satisfaction ultimately arises out of 'cultural' chances, not simply 'political' chances. The implication of the sociologists is that there are numerous children who, for reasons of class, are being unfairly inhibited from going on to the education they deserve. My point is that many of these children are, for cultural reasons, likely to be inhibited from gaining the best of what is offered them even if they were to be offered 'chances' in these terms; and this because they have already been formed by historical socio-cultural forces which makes the segment of 'high' culture put before them pretty meaningless—even their range of linguistic capacity inhibits them, as Dr. Bernstein has pointed out. History, as a famous sociologist once said, is not a bus you can get off at will. The mere indication of higher I.Q. does not, in itself, indicate ability to benefit from what is, in effect, for many children a foreign cultural experience. A great deal of social mobility has already been achieved, so that class barriers no longer constitute the inhibiting factors they once did; anyone of real ability can now make the grade, if that is the term for it. But an *excessive* concern for such opportunities may well be against the true educational interests of children of lesser, though still of good, ability who may, at the moment, seem to be stigmatized as 'social waste'. Their satisfactions may spring out of a fuller exploitation of such cultural possibilities as form part of their world rather than an attempt to afford them 'opportunities' via an unpalatable higher culture they cannot really assimilate. And this implies seeing the secondary modern schools (and the lower forms of comprehensive schools) not as places for the failures, nor schools in which a certain number of children are 'wrongly placed', but as schools which offer cultural opportunities for satisfactions within what is rapidly emerging as the characteristic cultural forms of twentieth-century man—the radio, cinema, TV and so on.[1] The whole notion of being wrongly placed helps to denigrate, subtly, these schools, the implication being that no-one with the slightest intelligence would want to go to them. If they could be afforded some cultural vitality in their own right there would need to be much less concern for possible 'misplacement'. Furthermore, a good deal of the 'wastage' that goes on at the moment at grammar school and university probably springs out of unpalatable cultural provision; and some of the so-called successes acquire only a veneer of high culture, a veneer sufficient to enable them to pass examinations, not one adequate to inform their actual living. Many of these would be better nurtured by a quite different sort of educational provision.

It is some such thinking about our educational problems that makes me regret current obsessions about class, which, interpreted in largely political terms, strikes me as a curiously outmoded centre of concern, relevant amidst the rigidities of the nineteenth century but hardly fundamental in view of today's fluidities. I do not mean to suggest that class does not play its part—it does, and always will. It is hardly reasonable to expect that a modern nation state of immense technical complexity can function without a power structure; and, once you get this, you also get social groupings which protect their own 'interests' by presenting a hostile front to possible encroachers and which come to accept a homogeneous set of values characteristic of social classes. The most that can be expected is a reasonable degree of mobility—and this, at least, has been achieved. Anything more is likely to meet simply the stubborn imperfectibility of human institutions; no human problem of this nature can be reduced below a certain level simply because it is a required and irreducible characteristic of complex societies. Indeed, in so far as class divisions lead to cultural heterogeneity, some degree of class division may be said to enrich the State.

[1] This, of course, only hints at what I have in mind. Cf. my *Education in an Industrial Society* for a fuller treatment.

My own priority for investigation is 'pop' culture. Here the social scientists are only just beginning to take over from the literary critics;[1] and, in so far as 'pop' culture drives straight to the affective core of the individual life, its power to make or mar individual life is much more potent than class. Give a man an adequate life experience—and what is culture about other than that?—make him truly individual and independent and the narrow jealousies implicit in class rivalry shrink in importance. Here, it seems to me, is a really important field for social investigation[2]; for 'opportunity' should be multifarious, not simply manifested in the chance to pursue one particular path to 'success'.

[1] Cf. J. D. Halloran's *Consent or Control* for an admirable summary of recent work in the social science field.

[2] Undertaken much more fully in the U.S.A. than in this country.

Educational Research: A Criticism

Part of our thinking about education has become highly technical in that it is served by a proliferation of research techniques designed to discover the *facts* of the educational situation; and these facts, of course, have their influence on the choices we make concerning what functions we think our schools ought to perform. The philosophical assumptions on which these techniques depend warrant, it seems to me, more investigation than they normally get. For we need to ask what sort of research is research into education.

Here I shall only be dealing with one sort—that implicit in the field of the social psychology of education. But it is necessary to realize, from the outset, that different sorts of questions invite different sorts of answers offering varying possibilities of validation and probability.

I

In recent years research in the psychosocial sciences has come in for considerable criticism. Adverse comment has been directed against the philosophical preconceptions in terms of which empirical research in these fields has been carried on, against particular imperfections in methodology, and on the grounds of the comparative triviality of both the matters which have received attention and of the results which have accrued. In so far as certain sorts of research in education employ procedures characteristic of research in the social sciences (and although the two fields are obviously by no means co-extensive, there is some overlap in that certain educational problems involve sociological or socially psychological factors), many of the criticisms directed against what goes on in the psychosocial sciences have their relevance in the educational field also. The nature of these criticisms, therefore, must be carefully examined. I must state straight away that it is with research in education of this kind that I shall be almost exclusively concerned in this article.

In education, as in the study of society generally, the claim is often made that investigation involves methods of research analagous to those employed in the natural sciences and that the findings can be established with a similar degree of certainty. Thus, for example, the Director of the National Foundation of Educational Research in England has said: 'Over the last sixty years or so, we have come to see that there are . . . educational *sciences* which, within their scope, are susceptible to scientific rigour as are the so-called exact and natural sciences.'[1] Yet Dr. Wall notes, in the fields susceptible to scientific investigation, the importance of large-scale enterprises undertaken by a team of researchers: 'The complexity of the variables with which we are faced in any real problem, coupled with the facts that the variation of one factor at a time and the destruction of experimental material, are impossible, make the educational sciences extremely precarious if they are not pursued by a well-equipped team. Moreover exact replication of experiments is impossible. Hence we are obliged to rely upon carefully chosen large samples, upon the closest possible estimates of statistical probability (rather than on exact demonstration) and upon a sufficient awareness of sources of error so that they can be randomised if not controlled or eliminated.'[2]

[1] W. D. Wall, 'Educational Research and the Needs of the Schools'. An address delivered at the Annual Conference of the National Association of Inspectors of Schools and Educational Organizers, 2nd October 1959 (London, National Association of Inspectors of Schools and Educational Organizers, 1959), p. 3.

[2] Ibid., p. 5.

Here he seems to be admitting that the educational sciences are not, in fact, 'as susceptible to scientific rigour as are the so-called exact and natural sciences'. But it is interesting to note the grounds on which he admits this. They are based on the complexity ('the variables') of the situations involved and on the fact that in many cases it is not possible to arrange experimental situations involving human beings. There is no suggestion that the nature of the basic 'material' of the educational or social sciences may often be different *in kind* from that investigated by the physical sciences. Yet it is on such grounds that the attack on current modes of research in the social sciences has been mounted. The attempt to assimilate the natural and the social sciences, it is urged, is fundamentally a mistake.

The situation has been admirably analysed recently by Mr. P. Winch: '. . . the notion of a human society involves a scheme of concepts which is logically incompatible with the kinds of explanation offered in the natural sciences.'[1] Winch analyses a classical exposition of this view that social phenomena are of the same order as physical, only very much more complicated and involving more variables. He demonstrates its falsity by showing that the natural scientist is governed by only one set of rules, those relevant to scientific investigation, whereas the social scientist has to take into account another set of rules as well, those involved in the 'phenomenon' he is investigating; for this phenomenon is itself a manifestation of social activity which will normally be subject to human purposes and meaning in a manner in which natural phenomena are not. This implies that the understanding of social phenomena involves a qualitatively different approach to that needed with natural, in that such understanding implies something more than simply external observation: it necessitates at least an imaginative projection into what the phenomena concerned mean, a meaning which can only come fully from inside the activity to be studied: '. . . a historian or sociologist of religion must himself have some religious feeling if he is to make sense of the religious movement

[1] P. Winch, *The Idea of a Social Science* (London, Routledge and Kegan Paul, 1958), p. 72.

he is studying. . . . A historian must have some aesthetic sense if he is to understand the problems confronting the artists of his period; and without this he will have left out of his account precisely what would have made it a history of *art*, as opposed to a rather puzzling external account of certain motions which certain people have been perceived to go through.'[1]

Mr. Winch's analysis of social phenomena[2] has been considerably influenced by the concept of *Verstehen* adopted by Max Weber and other German social theorists. Quentin Gibson, in his recent book,[3] refers to this concept as involving 'a sympathetic understanding of our fellowmen, of finding a meaning in their activities, of grasping intuitively how they feel, what their plans are, what they are driving at'. He denies, however, that such 'sympathetic understanding 'can provide us 'with any evidence of an alternative kind' to that supplied empirically, i.e., that 'obtained from our sensory observations of the world around us or from our awareness of our own mental processes'.[4] He does not deny that participating in a social process may be valuable as a means to understanding; but to do so, he considers, simply places the investigator in a 'peculiarly favourable position to give evidence'; it does not open up to him sources of evidence different *in kind* from that available to others: 'Unless the anthropologist becomes accepted by the members of the tribe, there are many things he will not hear about. Unless he is in a position to observe the daily round of inconspicuous activities, he will not have the material from which to infer beliefs and attitudes.'[5] But, surely, it is not simply a matter of the "things he will not hear about'; it is a question of the meanings that are to be attached to what he does know about. A social act takes on meaning from the subjective understanding of a personality participating within a specific framework and may differ in

[1] Ibid., p. 88.

[2] He has other important points to make about the possibilities of prediction and the role of generalization.

[3] Cf. Quentin Gibson, *The Logic of Social Enquiry* (London, Routledge and Kegan Paul, 1960).

[4] Ibid., pp. 47–8.

[5] Ibid., p. 51.

significance in accordance with depth of penetrative comprehension. Even when the general character of religious practices is recognized as such, the 'meaning' they may have to the believer can play a quite different role in the life of that believer from what they can in that of a non-believer. In the same way, the act of sex can 'mean' anything from the semi-clinical ('relief of tension') to the semi-mystical ('She is all States, and all Princes, I. . . .').[1]

It may be urged that, even so, our knowledge would still ultimately rest on observation or awareness of our own mental processes.

This may be so; but it is not the point at issue. The significance of the notion of *Verstehen* lies in the way it helps us to appreciate how understanding the social and the natural world may differ. In the case of the latter, we only need to impose our concepts on the regularities observed; in the case of the former, such regularities as are observed take on meaning in relation not to the concepts *we* employ to distinguish them but to the social meanings they already have independently of our observation. It is so that we may arrive at the second order of meaning that 'sympathetic understanding' is important. It might, of course, still be argued that the 'true' participant understands things which the social scientist who participates only to understand misses —that in the very act of our self-awareness of our own mental activities, we separate ourselves from the unself-conscious experience. And, of course, in what follows I certainly do not wish to deny that much knowledge may be gained by purely external observation, or that there are, for instance, 'psychosocial phenomena which are repeated in time and space and lend themselves to statistical mass observation'—such as 'the ever-repeated mass phenomena of births, deaths, marriages, divorces' and so on.

[1] Indeed, one of the difficulties about social investigation is that certain sorts of experience belong, socially, only to a few, though there may be elements within the experience common to mankind—as in sex relationships. Hence the tendency, in so much social investigation, to treat experience at a comparatively crude level; the act of sex, in such investigations, is usually reduced to its common physiological element.

The above quotation is from Professor P. Sorokin's recent attack on current methods in sociology.[1] This is a book which obviously needs to be treated with a good deal of caution, as it is frequently intemperate and unbalanced. Nevertheless it contains numerous acute criticisms of modern techniques of psycho-social investigation. Sorokin, indeed, divides social phenomena into two broad categories: what he terms 'congeries', chance collocations of unrelated social phenomena similar in kind to the mass phenomena cited above, and 'systems', in which the relationships of the parts are of a qualitatively different nature, corresponding to the organic meaning structure implicit in the phenomenon concerned. Such 'systems' are understood not through external observation but through 'direct co-feeling and co-experiencing': 'Only through direct empathy . . . can one grasp the essential nature and difference between a criminal gang and a fighting battalion; between a harmonious and a broken family. . . . The same can be said of the nature and differences of religious, scientific, aesthetic, ethical, legal, economic, technological, and other cultural value-systems and their subsystems. Without the direct living experience of these cultural values, they will remain *terra incognita* for our outside observer and statistical analyst.'[1] In support of his views on intuition he even cites current practice in the natural sciences themselves, where intuition has an important part to play; and concludes that 'the anti-intuitional and anti-

[1] P. A. Sorokin, *Fads and Foibles in Modern Sociology* (Chicago, Henry Regnery, 1956).

[2] Ibid., pp. 159–60. Sorokin has many other criticisms to offer—notably about the basis of mental testing (cf. his 'Testomania', *Harvard Educational Review*, XXV (Fall, 1955), 199–213), the emphasis on quantitative methods, the deficiencies of supposedly 'experimental methods' and the use of controls, and the drawbacks inherent in questionnaire methods. He is particularly contemptuous of 'speech-reactional operations', the lack of adequate definition of terms, the deficiencies of investigations into group behaviour, where some of the studies at least are 'more dull and vague than a description of the case by a competent novelist or an imaginative participant-observer', and the fallacy of expecting precise prediction in this field. All of these have their relevance to the sorts of techniques, methods and expectations arising from research in the educational fields.

rational position of our psychosocial empiricists is obsolescent'.

Yet, of course, reliance on 'intuition' has its grave dangers; one is reminded of Karl Popper's tart comment: 'By their intuition some people are prevented from even imagining that anybody can possibly dislike chocolate.' And certainly, intuition works better when controlled by the known facts; the intuition of the *natural* scientist, which plays its part in the formation of hypotheses, nevertheless works within the framework created by the discipline of investigation involved. The question now arises as to how the social scientist, in view of the complexity of the situation by which he is faced—a complexity, be it noted, which is not reducible simply to a question of 'variables' in the sense in which that word would be applicable in the physical sphere—can manipulate his concepts. He cannot simply 'arrange' the external world so as to accord with the traditions of his undertaking, for that part of the external world in which he is interested has its own set of meanings, and without some cognizance of those meanings in and for themselves, his undertaking would be fruitless. Further, such concepts may involve problems of value, about which agreement is likely to be difficult to achieve.

One of the most interesting solutions to the problem of how meaning-structures which contain a subjective or evaluative element can be made in some measure objective for scientific investigation is that suggested by the late Alfred Schutz (Schuetz). Schutz accepts the difference between the physical and social worlds and urges that the task of the social sciences is 'to develop methodological devices for attaining objective and verifiable knowledge of a subjective meaning structure'. His aim methodologically is not to rely exclusively on 'empathy' or intuitive understanding but to clarify conceptually how the interpretative subjective understanding men practice in their daily lives in the common-sense world can be harnessed to the requirements of what he insists is a *science*. Hence he refers to the 'erroneous conclusion that the social sciences are *toto coelo* different from the natural sciences, a view which disregards the fact that certain procedural rules relating to correct thought organisation are common to all empirical sciences'.[1] And he refutes the doctrine of what he terms 'sensationalistic empiricism . . . which identifies experience with sensory observation and which assumes that the only alternative to controllable and, therefore, objective sensory observation is that of subjective and, therefore, uncontrollable and unverifiable introspection'.[2]

Schutz derives much of his positive theory from a refinement of this concept of *Verstehen*, which he translates as 'Interpretative Understanding'. He begins by considering in some detail how in common-sense experience we arrive, in the world of inter-subjectivity which is the social world, at an 'understanding' of each other. He considers that *Verstehen* simply refers to that understanding of each other at which we arrive by common sense and social acculturation in the ordinary course of events. Furthermore, there are many social situations where what appears to be the privacy of the individual is subject to the publicly verifiable and accountable rules of procedure controlling the nature of the experience concerned. In illustration he offers the discussions of a trial jury, where the 'rules of procedure' are furnished by the 'rules of evidence', as controlling elements. It is this 'exploration of the general principles according to which man in daily life organizes his experiences, and especially those of the social world' which 'is the first task of the methodology of the social sciences'.[3] Central to the solution of this task is the notion of typicality, with the opportunity it affords for some degree of generalization.

'Typification' involves an abstraction from the concrete world around one made for the particular purpose in hand. 'Objects' are invested with meaning in accordance with these purposes. These meanings are in the last resort known to the actors. But in so far as their actions form part of the social world, they are

[1] Alfred Schuetz, 'Common-sense and Scientific Interpretation of Human Action', *Philosophy and Phenomenological Research*, XIV (September, 1953), p. 4. I am grateful to Dr. Asher Tropp for drawing my attention to the work of Schutz.

[2] Alfred Schutz, 'Concept and Theory Formation in the Social Sciences', *The Journal of Philosophy*, LI (29th April 1954), p. 261.

[3] Ibid., p. 267.

open to the same sort of common sense interpretation as has been noted above—something which in daily life we all accomplish frequently. It may therefore be impossible to understand fully the subjective meanings people infuse into their actions (a point which, incidentally, a reading of Joseph Conrad would reinforce), but they can be understood in their typicality; thus: '. . . the social scientist replaces the thought objects of common sense thought relating to unique events and occurrences by constructing a model of a sector of the social world within which merely those typified events occur that are relevant to the scientist's particular problem under scrutiny. [In order to do this, he constructs] typical patterns of the actors' motives and ends, even of their attitudes and personalities, of which their actual conduct is just an instance or example.'[1] These are the first level constructs, involving the notion of subjective interpretation, on which the second level constructs of the social sciences have been built up. The difficulty now is: all scientific explanations of the social world must involve these subjective meanings; but, to be scientific, their propositions must be subject to verification and not refer simply to private uncontrollable experience. In other words, how is it possible 'to form objective concepts and an objectively verifiable theory of subjective meaning-structure?'[2]

The answer lies in the construction of models—'homunculi'—in terms of which the social situation can be 'interpreted'.[3] 'The basic insight that the constructs formed by the social scientist are constructs of the constructs formed in common-sense thinking by the actors on the social scene offers an answer.'[4] These scientific constructs are 'ideal typical constructs' created as part of the scientist's procedural rules with regard to relevance, thus ensuring the objectivity of the investigation. How are they arrived at? The social scientist '. . . observes certain facts and events within social reality which refer to human action patterns from what he has observed. Thereupon he co-

[1] Ibid., p. 268.

[2] Ibid., p. 270.

[3] This notion of 'homunculi' has, of course, been much influenced by Max Weber's concept of the Ideal Type.

[4] Schutz, op. cit., p. 270.

ordinates to these typical course-of-action patterns models of an ideal actor or actors, whom he imagines as being gifted with consciousness. Yet it is a consciousness restricted so as to contain nothing but the elements relevant to the performing of the course-of-action patterns observed. He thus ascribes to this fictitious consciousness a set of typical notions, purposes, goals, which are assumed to be invariant in the specious consciousness of the imaginary actor-model. This homunculus or puppet is supposed to be interrelated in interaction patterns to other homunculi or puppets constructed in a similar way. Among these homunculi with which the social scientist populates his model of the social world of everyday life, sets of motives, goals, roles—in general, systems of relevances—are distributed in such a way as the scientific problems under scrutiny require. Yet . . . these constructs are by no means arbitrary. They are subject to the postulate of consistency and to the postulate of adequacy. The latter means that each term in such a scientific model of human action must be constructed in such a way that a human act performed within the real world by an individual actor as indicated by the typical construct would be understandable to the actor himself as well as to his fellowmen in terms of common-sense interpretation of every-day life. Compliance with the postulate of logical consistency warrants the objective validity of the thought objects constructed by the social scientist; compliance with the postulate of adequacy warrants their compatibility with the constructs of everyday life.'[1] Thus can subjective meanings be objectified for the purpose of scientific investigation.

In the creation of homunculi I can add a refinement on my own account. A training in literature is of great assistance in the sensitizing of the intelligence to the complexities of social life and to the psychological reactions of individuals in social situa-

[1] Further detailed account of these 'homunculi' will be found in 'Common sense and Scientific Interpretation', pp. 31–3. And the criteria operative in their creation—relevance, adequacy, logical consistency and compatibility —are discussed in Alfred Schuetz 'The Social World and the Theory of Social Action', *Research*, XXVII (Summer, 1960), pp. 220–1.

tions, in that literature uniquely affords the feel of the 'whole man alive', as D. H. Lawrence pointed out. The literary intelligence can do much to refine the comparatively crude notions of personalities employed in educational research by affording the subjective element in the creation of homunculi width and depth and at the same time by admitting that notion of universality which is an acknowledged criterion of great literature. Researchers, indeed, could do worse than to study the *Notebooks* of Henry James or *The Art of the Novel*. To be specific, what I have in mind is the sort of sensibility cultivated by the artist in relation to his 'characters'—represented, for instance, by Turgenev's desire, quoted by James, '. . . to show my people, to exhibit their relations with each other; for that is all my measure. If I watch them long enough, I see them come together, I see them *placed*, I see them engaged in this or that act, in this or that difficulty. How they look and move and speak and behave, always in the setting I have found for them, is my account of them . . .' together with James's subsequent comments in the preface to *The Portrait of a Lady*. Such insight, controlled by Schutz's postulates of relevance, adequacy, logical consistency and compatibility, offers a step in the direction of a refinement of type creation.[1]

Before I attempt to illustrate by the actual examination of some pieces of educational research how some of the foregoing principles might be applied, there is one final methodological point to be made. Despite some attempts in that direction, the discipline of social research has not succeeded in creating a specialized language of its own; indeed, in view of the nature of its subject matter which, as I have emphasized, is unlike that of the physical sciences in that it deals with what already has meaning apart from that assigned to it by the scientist, it is possible that the social sciences will never succeed in creating a fully technical vocabulary. Since, then, the statement of research topics usually involves the use of words common in everyday usage, the prime requisite in the consideration of research prob-

[1] On the role of the literary intelligence in education, see my 'Education and the Literary Intelligence' reprinted in this volume (chapter 2).

lems is the conceptual clarification of the terms employed, at least to the extent that possible ambiguities are cleared up or that ostensive definitions are offered. Extended clarifications of the type I have in mind can be found in R. S. Peters's *The Concept of Motivation* and in other books in the valuable series of 'Studies in Philosophical Psychology' to which Professor Peters's book belongs. A recent article in the *Harvard Educational Review* on research into the relative effectiveness of teacher- and learner-centred methods in education reveals the immense wastage which springs from a failure to analyse adequately the concepts of 'democratic' and 'authoritarian' teaching respectively.[1] It is disturbing to find how little modern philosophical techniques of linguistic analysis and clarification have affected our thinking about social science research; yet as a preliminary to any such research it is important at least to decide what questions involved are really conceptual and what empirical. As Winch observes: '. . . many of the more important theoretical issues which have been raised in [social science studies] belong to philosophy rather than to science and are, therefore, to be settled by a priori conceptual analysis rather than by empirical research. For example, the question of what constitutes social behaviour is a demand for an elucidation of the *concept* of social behaviour. In dealing with questions of this sort there should be no question of "waiting to see" what empirical research will show us; it is a matter of tracing the implications of the concept we use.'[2]

II

It is necessary to see how the methodological notions we have been examining might affect our assessment of some contem-

[1] Richard C. Anderson, 'Learning in Discussions: A Resume of the Authoritarian-Democratic Studies', *Harvard Educational Review*, XXIX (Summer, 1959), pp. 201–15.

[2] Cf. P. Winch, op. cit., p. 17.

porary educational research. I will take most of my examples from the journal, *Educational Research*, where the articles concerned draw extensively on research undertaken in the United States as well as in England.

One omission which can frequently be noted lies in the neglect of an adequate clarification of the concepts employed. Thus Dr. Kellmer Pringle, in the article, 'Social Learning and Its Measurement'[1] becomes involved with the extremely difficult conceptual problem as to what constitutes 'social maturity'. She opens her article with the surprising remark that 'The adult who is socially mature is not hard to recognize,' and proceeds to list five broad characteristics, each of which merits further analysis of its own account. She then comes to appreciate that 'the general concept of social maturity and the more specific one of social competence, are crucial for psychological study' and proceeds to offer a tentative definition in terms of conformity to social custom and of constructive participation in community affairs, a definition which she admits 'begs fundamental questions'. She shrugs off criticism with the remark that further 'argument would lead into moral and philosophical realms outside the scope of this article' and continues as if conformity to the standards laid down by society were the sole mark of the mature personality, though she does admit that these standards may vary from social group to social group.

Obviously, from what she says in the rest of the article, she favours attempts to measure levels of social 'competence' which she considers essential elements in the development of social maturity. 'By this term is meant the ability to carry out social tasks normally achieved by children of a given age as there are some fields in which all children are expected to reach eventually certain minimum standards. Examples of such fields are habits of eating, cleanliness, dressing, the attainment of personal and economic independence.'[2] This represents an entirely arbitrary selection from a possible range of characteristics as measur-

[1] M. L. Kellmer Pringle, 'Social Learning and its Measurement', *Educational Research*, II (June, 1960), pp. 194–206.

[2] Ibid., pp. 199–200.

ing instruments; moreover, some of these characteristics are themselves subject to wide possibilities of interpretation. What, for instance, constitutes 'personal and economic independence'?

The fact is, that research along these lines is impossible given the vagueness of the concepts to be 'measured'; and there is a further danger that what will be produced will simply be a number of stereotypes of behaviour which will militate against the recognition of children who, perhaps because of superior ability, demonstrate certain social oddities. As Dr. Wall puts it in the previous number of *Educational Research*, in talking of 'Highly Intelligent Children': 'Some of the problems of these children . . . arise from deeply-rooted attitudes in our society, stereotypes of what is and is not acceptable from children and adolescents' (ibid., pp. 199–200).

A further example will reinforce the necessity for such conceptual analysis and, at the same time, indicate how Schutz's approach may be of assistance as a technique of research.[1] In an article by Dr. K. M. Evans, it is concluded that, though '. . . there is a great deal of information available about teachers and teaching efficiency. . . . Some of it is contradictory and some of it inconclusive. Differences between results obtained appear to be more marked than similarities. . . .'[2] This is not an impressive result in a matter as fundamental to the process of education as the effectiveness of the teacher, particularly in view of the 'very large number of investigations which have been carried out'. When one has read Dr. Evans's article, however, it is not difficult to see where some, at least, of the trouble has arisen. She stresses the importance of agreement about the criteria in terms of which what constitutes 'good' teaching is to be

[1] I have been led to make some slight modifications to the original wording of this section as a result of an article by Professor J. R. Martin: 'Can there be universally applicable Criteria of Good Teaching' (*Harvard Educational Review*, Vol. 33, No, 4, Fall, 1963). The issue between us seems to depend on a willingness to accept that 'teaching' can be a monadic, dyadic, tetradic term as well as a triadic.

[2] K. M. Evans, 'Research on Teaching Ability', *Educational Research*, II (June 1959), p. 33.

judged. What, however, she, and those whose work she considers, fail to recognize is that before the question of criteria can even be raised it is necessary to undertake a conceptual clarification of what it means to teach, what, in fact, is involved in the concept of 'teaching'. The search for criteria all too often is regarded as a purely empirical matter, as Dr. Evans herself makes clear when she introduces her own search for criteria by asking: 'How do we, in fact, assess teaching ability, and are our methods satisfactory?' But there is the prior question of what constitutes the process of teaching someone something which is not in itself an empirical question; it is a request for a clarification of what is involved, conceptually, in the activity of teaching. We must be clear about what constitutes the ability we are supposed to be assessing. Furthermore, of course, the elucidation of what it means when we speak of 'teaching' implies that the teaching has been successful, for it is not possible at the same time both to teach someone something and to fail to teach someone something. The notion of teaching unsuccessfully involves a contradiction in terms, though, of course, it is possible to talk of 'having tried to teach'; and it is possible to distinguish degrees of success.[1]

When we speak of 'teaching' we imply, as part of the grammar of the concept, both a direct and an indirect object—we teach something to someone; no process just of 'teaching' is possible. To summarize what should, by rights, be argued at some length, it would be reasonable to conclude that, by such a concept, we imply the conscious bringing about in others of certain desirable mental or dispositional changes by morally acceptable means. It is necessary to insist on the moral reputableness of the means in order to cut out changes brought about by torture, brain-washing, etc. It is also necessary to insist that the changes shall be desirable, as otherwise teachers like Fagin

[1] Dr. Israel Scheffler, in his recent *The Language of Education* (Illinois, Thomas, 1960), distinguishes between the 'success' and 'intentional' use of the word 'teaching'. Even if one were to accept this rather than a distinction between 'teaching' and 'teaching' (i.e., an elliptical form implying 'trying to teach') it is obvious that, in considering teaching ability, one has the 'success' meaning in mind.

would qualify. Of course, it would be possible to dispute the adequacy of the definition—conceptual questions are not ones that can be 'settled' in the way in which, frequently, empirical ones can. Nevertheless, the analysis has been carried out far enough to make clear some, at least, of the logic of the concept of 'teaching'.

For the sake of argument, then, let it be agreed that the success of a teacher is to be measured in terms of the degree of desirable change he can bring about in the understanding or dispositional abilities of his pupils. The point now arises as to how these changes are to be measured. And here it becomes obvious that there is no possibility of setting up any general test of competence. The tests must take account of the nature of the change involved. In the same way, it is only possible to construct a model of successful teaching in relation to the teaching of a particular 'subject' in terms of insight into the *nature* of that particular 'subject' and of the particular sorts of demands that the nature of the 'subject' makes in relation to the stage of development of the pupils concerned. For, if the successful teacher is he who makes those specific changes in his charges which relate most closely to the fundamental structure of the 'subject' concerned, taking into account their particular stage of development, it is obvious that 'subjects' differ immensely in the nature of the demands which they are likely to make on the teacher's capacity. Hence the model of the successful teacher, the 'homunculus' in Schutz's terminology, must to some extent differ according to subject and pupils. Thus, to give an example, it is no good even setting up the possession of a good voice as a universal requisite for all types of teaching. Even apart from the ambiguity as to what constitutes a 'good' voice, it is clear that voice, in the teacher of poetry, with its demands on reading and dramatic ability, is likely to be more important than it is in, say, a teacher of woodwork; and clarity of enunciation is likely to be much more vital in a teacher of foreign languages than it is in one of history.

My point is that there are no fruitful universally applicable criteria of what constitutes a good teacher; and the attempt to lay down such general criteria is, in part, an explanation of the unproductiveness of much of the research on the subject which has been done. What, then, is required as a preliminary to research is an initial clarification of the basic concepts employed. Once teaching is seen as an interactive process in a context, it is relevant to demand insight into the particular nature of the interactions involved in different sorts of context. It is useless to draw up lists of 'characteristics' and then to try to measure how important each is. Some of these characteristics may enter into all the contexts where good teaching takes place,[1] but the emphasis to be placed on each will vary with the nature of the specific kind of teaching situation involved; furthermore, such characteristics will be analysable only in relation to a total configuration which will bring into prominence now one aspect, now another. The only way to scientific understanding of such a complex situation lies in the creation of a series of models based in some measure on subjective assessments of objective situations—what it *means* to teach this in this sort of context. There can be no useful general answer to the question 'What makes a good teacher?' because a good teacher is always acting

[1] For example, intelligence. As soon as one begins to look at what is involved in teaching contexts in the way I have suggested, one comes to see how complex the situation usually is. For instance, what for many years has appeared to be a fairly mechanical job, that of teaching the first steps in arithmetic, is shown, if the theories of Piaget and Dr. Dienes are correct, to be a much more complicated matter than was thought; in that what is really necessary is not simply the drilling of mechanical steps but a series of explanations which will clarify not only the processes at stake but help to make clear to the child the very nature of the mathematical concepts involved. Yet Dr. Evans informs us that 'Results of statistical studies . . . leave the question of the importance of intelligence in some doubt. In many studies correlations between the results of intelligence tests and assessments of teaching efficiency are small.' But this surely simply raises doubts about the relevance of intelligence tests in relation to intelligent behaviour. For 'intelligence' is not a quality we can have apart from the ability to act intelligently. When we say that a human being shows intelligence, we don't mean that he applies something called 'intelligence' and then behaves; we mean that he displays intelligence by his ability to act successfully (whatever that may mean in the context) in situations requiring a complex interplay of understanding and judgment. When teaching situations are analysed in the way I have suggested this surely is likely to be characteristic of most.

in concrete situations which will vary the demands made upon his skill; at best, there can be a number of particular requirements to meet broadly assessed similarities of situation. Built into the very notion of teaching is the need to consider: 'Who is teaching what to whom?' Here, Schutz's conceptual apparatus of the 'homunculus' is of the first importance[1]—as, even in general terms, it helped in seeing what is wrong with so many attempts to define the nature of the 'good teacher'. At the very least one needs to create 'homunculi' called 'the French teacher'' 'the history teacher' or the 'nursery school teacher', and to assess typically how these conceive of their jobs in certain recurrent contexts.

Something of the same way of looking at the situation, involving a more strongly marked appreciation of the subjective element, may be shown to have its uses in relation to Dr. C. M. Fleming's study of 'Class Size as a Variable in the Teaching Situation'.[2] Fleming points out that, contrary to expectation, 'The benefits of small classes, though commonly taken for granted by theorists, are as yet largely undemonstrated in the pages of accredited research reports. This conclusion has been reached at every level from infant-school to University lecture-theatre. It has been formulated in relation to many subjects; and it is supported both by test results and by assessments of various types.'[3]

The interesting thing about the researches that Dr. Fleming analyses is the small amount of attention that appears to be paid to what could reasonably be predicted concerning the subjective interpretation the teachers concerned are likely to place on the nature of their job. Implicit in every effort, it can reasonably be assumed, is a certain interpretation of what each one was

[1] It should be said that Dr. Evans is by no means unaware of some of these difficulties (cf. Section II, 'The assessment of teaching'). But she points to general difficulties resting on empirical grounds; she fails to see the initial need for conceptual analysis, and she suggests no conceptual tool by means of which the difficulties may be in some measure overcome.

[2] C. M. Fleming, 'Class Size as a Variable in the Teaching Situation', *Educational Research*, I (February 1959), pp. 35–48.

[3] Ibid., p. 38.

about, i.e., that implicit in the concept of teaching which we have already examined above. In other words, whatever the 'variables' might seem to be, the total situation is likely to be controlled by the teacher's realization that it is his function to teach something to a set, large or small, of somebodies. This, at least, is the unspoken assumption of his enterprise. That being so, it is not expecting too much to suggest that the teacher, in various small ways, would adapt himself to the nature of the task in front of him, particularly when he would know he was in a test situation. Adaptations of voice, vigour, clarity of enunciation, and so on would take place—anyone who has taught or lectured to both small and large groups knows how different the 'feel' of the two situations is and how that difference of 'feel' affects the actual 'teaching' in a number of subtle ways, even though superficially the 'methods' adopted in the two cases may appear on the surface exactly similar.[1] Thus the element of size cannot simply be regarded as a 'variable' in the sense in which a physical phenomenon can be so regarded in a physical experiment, where the 'subjective' response of the other 'variables' is nonexistent; it is a 'variable' which leads to a qualitative difference among the other variables', a 'variable', that is, which alters the 'meaning' of the situation in ways which affect conduct qualitatively; and this is quite frequent in the consideration of 'variables' in psychosocial phenomena, for the variables themselves are invested with subjective meaning and cannot be treated simply as 'factors' with their monolithic implications. In one experiment Fleming reports on, the clue to the situation is perhaps there; but its implications seem to have been missed. Fleming first attempts to treat the mechanical 'variables' involved: 'In extensive interviews in which an attempt was made to discover the opinions of the students on such matters as

[1] This is a different matter from those 'subtleties of interpersonal relationships' which Dr. Fleming notes at the end of her article, which seem only to involve differences of approach—teacher- or learner-centred—not a difference of the 'feel' of a situation springing from a similarity of subjective assessment of the task involved within the *same* approach. (It is stressed in some of the reports that the same methods had to be used in the various test situations.)

vision, hearing, ventilation, opportunities for questions, the large groups appeared to have been as satisfactory as the small except for some complaints as to overcrowding. . . .'[1] However, a crucial element in the situation is hinted at but not taken up —or so the report would seem to signify: 'The teachers, on interview, expressed awareness of greater effort in establishing informality with large groups, in enlisting participation in discussion and in discovering special difficulties among students. . . .'[2] The situation, indeed, is analogous to the famous Hawthorne experiment when two groups of girls were chosen for an investigation into factory conditions; the physical conditions of the experimental group were altered in order to assess the importance of a variety of variables in working conditions, whilst those of the control group remained constant. It was discovered that, in these circumstances, such physical variables were unimportant; what mattered was the attention paid to the girls, so that output in both control and experimental groups advanced equally. In other words, the girls' subjective interpretation of the importance of their work had altered: by asking their help and co-operation, the company had made the girls feel important, and their whole attitude to work had changed. This factor of subjective interpretation proved much more important than all the physical variables involved.

Another situation in which it is possible to employ Schutz's conception of the homunculus is in the assessment of the adequacy of questionnaire techniques and in the criticism of specific questions in particular pieces of social and educational research, as well as in the initial refinement of question-setting techniques. One social phenomenon who merits investigation but who has not received the attention he deserves is the question-answerer. A good deal of attention has been focused on the refinement of questioning techniques—avoidance of ambiguities, development of multi-choice or 'open-ended' questions, inventories—and so on. Attention has been paid to layout, clarity of instructions, attractiveness of appearance, etc. But much less attempt has been made to analyse the processes implicit in the actual under-

[1] Fleming, op. cit., p. 45. [2] Ibid.

taking of questionnaire-solving—the sort of psychic expectations with which it is approached, the nature of the attention which is likely to be given to the question; what, in fact, it is likely to *mean* to a typical questionnaire-solver to be faced by questions of the conventional type for information-finding.

One point which might become clear as a result of an attempt to create such an image of an answerer is the fact that question-answering is a largely rational activity, one which, by the very nature of the demands it makes, the sort of attention it invites, involves only certain aspects of the personality—those associated with 'thinking things out', 'giving careful consideration to' and the like. This approach would imply the shutting-off of the less disciplined, more emotionally oriented aspects of human personality which, in the conventions of question-answering, are not likely to have much of a look in.

Let me try to illustrate my point by reference to a large-scale piece of research carried out by the Nuffield Foundation in England on the effects television viewing has on children.[1] The researchers attempted to discover something of the effect television had on children's values—the views of society, conceptions of adult life, ideas about foreigners and so on. One of their fields of interest was the ideas about marriage children imbibed from the TV screen, especially from the plays: 'We also tried to find out whether television affected the child's ideas as to what makes a good husband or wife. The children were asked to complete the following two sentences: *A good husband is a man who . . .* and *A good wife is a woman who . . .*'.[2]

In so far as a great deal of popular culture is concerned with love and marriage, the effect which the presentation of marital themes has on the young is one of the profoundest importance. Yet the questions barely skim the surface of the sort of interest which is likely to be aroused about the relations between the sexes. Furthermore, and of greater significance for the point I

[1] H. T. Himmelweit *et al.*, *Television and the Child* (London, Oxford University Press, 1958).

[2] Ibid., p. 247. The treatment is, in fact, very perfunctory for so important an aspect of the investigation.

am making, the very nature of the questions asks for an abstract, 'rational', common-sense type of answer remote from precisely that sort of affective impact that television is likely to make. Symptomatically, the investigators ask 'whether television affected the child's *ideas* as to what makes . . .'. They surely should have recognized the nature of television drama's appeal, an appeal which is remote from the rationalistic-moralistic ('good' wife) interest of the question asked. The sort of information that is needed here cannot be got at by questioning in this way, precisely because the whole psychic atmosphere in which such questions are answered is inimical to obtaining it. In other words, one's appreciation of the mental and psychological preconceptions of question-answering, one's re-creation, as it were, of the typical subjective responses of someone in the questionnaire-answering situation, makes one appreciate that questionnaires are only suitable for finding certain sorts of information ('for how long did you watch television last evening?') and are not likely to elicit useful results when affectively based responses are called for. The answer to the question '*A good husband is a man who* . . .' can probably only be superficially verbalized by adolescents anyway; and when the aim of the questions is to discover the effect of experiences which are themselves emotional in origin, the information gleaned is of only a very limited sort of interest.

Questionnaire-setters have usually assumed that their questions *can* be answered provided they are unambiguous, clearly phrased, etc. What they have insufficiently defined are the limitations involved in the very activity of question-answering which is, in fact, a very particular kind of undertaking. We need, that is, to know much more about the subjective attitudes and expectations of question-answerers. One wonders in how many pieces of research the neglect of similar subjective interpretation of the situation is not commented on or even remarked. At least, the fuller realization of its importance might do something to amend the present unsatisfactory state of research in education.

1961

Index

Index

Index

Index